What C

"If the church is to ~~...~~ ~~evangelization~~, she must multiply. Addition is not enough. *The Ministry Multiplication Cycle* captures the strategy of multiplication used by Jesus and reproduced by the apostles to reach the entire known world with the gospel in their lifetimes. The book provides not only the biblical basis but also the practical application for us to do the same today."

—ED STETZER
Executive Director,
Billy Graham Center of Evangelism

"Church planting and church multiplication are keys to ministry explosion. As you read and study this book on the Great Commission you will find that Christ wanted Christians to be equipped and to maximize their God-given potential for the kingdom."

—JOHN MAXWELL
CEO/President, Equip International

"Bill has been a friend of mine for many years and what exudes from him most is his passion for fulfilling the Great Commission. While many American Evangelicals enjoy the training table, the film room, and the practice sessions, Bill has always gone beyond preparation; he likes being in the game itself. I find that spirit both exemplary and contagious. His latest book reflects that—and perhaps that takeaway is what the American church as a whole can learn most from him and his writings."

—RALPH DROLLINGER
Teacher of the White House Cabinet Bible Study;
President and Founder, Capitol Ministries

"Bill Jones is a man of the Bible. What I love about Dr. Jones is that he not only knows the Scripture so well but applies it to real life in ministry with amazing results. As he says in this new book, 'If the

Bible teaches us what to believe and how to live, doesn't it seem reasonable that it just might teach us how to minister?' The answer is yes! The ministry multiplication strategy of Jesus in this book is a brilliant compilation of New Testament best practices and can work in any culture."

—HANS FINZEL
Leadership Mentor and author of
Top Ten Mistakes Leaders Make

"When you stop and pondered Jesus' parable of the sower, don't you wonder what it would be like to be the good soil that produces hundredfold? What would it take, how would I need to grow or surrender? Bill Jones' book *The Ministry Multiplication Cycle* provides us with a detailed, compelling look at Jesus' ministry, as a model for our lives to produce one hundred times. Having watched Bill in action and served some of the same leaders together, I see these principles lived out in his daily life. This is not just an interesting study for Bill. It takes time to tell if soil is going to produce a great crop, and I see God multiplying the fruit in Bill's life."

—LLOYD REEB
Founding Partner, Halftime Institute; author of
From Success to Significance and *Halftime for Couples*

"God has used Bill Jones' work to be a modern fulfillment of Ephesians 4:12. *The Ministry Multiplication Cycle* will equip a new generation of believers to reach the world for Christ. Grounded in a proper historical view of Scripture, through ingenious exegesis, Bill moves from great detail to the very practical in this work, making many deep concepts accessible to all who have a heart for evangelism. I am so excited to see the impact of this incredible work and heartily endorse it as a must-read for all believers from those focused on rubber-meets-the-road evangelism to the academic. You will not be disappointed; you will be changed!"

—LARRY GRIFFITH
CEO, Corporate Chaplains of America

"I respect Bill Jones' intellect. As an educator and leader, he has reached the apex of success in Christian higher education. But what I truly love about Bill is his passion for the gospel and the church. It's a zeal that has been tested and tried over the decades on the mission field as well as in the pulpit and the classroom. Who better than a true practitioner to write about multiplication and church planting than a man who has put his feet and his hand to the plow, gotten his hands dirty in the fields, and has the callouses to prove his love for the work of the gospel? I commend this book to you with great enthusiasm for the message it contains and great admiration for the man who is the vessel God is using to shape the future of the church and missions."

—**CLAYTON KING**
Teaching Pastor, NewSpring Church; evangelist and author

"In *The Ministry Multiplication Cycle* Bill Jones gives a biblical, practical, and comprehensive process for advancing the kingdom. I've been privileged to spend time with leaders of Crossover Global and affirm they are authentically putting this strategy into practice and seeing fruit. Bill has been teaching this for years, but it isn't academic theory. It's a proven model of a Jesus approach to unleashing the church."

—**STEVE MOORE**
President, Nexleader; author of
The Top 10 Leadership Conversations in the Bible

What Mission Leaders Are Saying

"This new book combines Bill Jones' passions—deep biblical reflection and practical field ministry. An approach that has been used to plant over two thousand churches among unreached peoples over the last twenty-five years, this work will be a great practical help to twenty-first-century global church planters."

—**ED SMITHER**
President, Evangelical Missiological Society

"The enormity of the task ahead requires us to think and act with multiplication as an expectation. Multiplication was what the first-century church experienced. Straightforward and easy to understand, Dr. Bill Jones captures simple yet profound steps toward multiplication."

—TED ESLER
President, Missio Nexus

"The book is an easy-to-read resource that will help you catch a biblically guided process for reaching, mentoring, and multiplying Jesus-followers globally. Bill Jones will make you think, and rethink, your assumptions about Jesus—both the how and why he did what he did. He will give you tools you can use and pass on as you teach and train others. If you choose not to follow what's here, I hope you have a better plan than this."

—GREG PARSONS
Director of Global Connections, Frontier Ventures
(formerly U.S. Center for World Mission)

"Missionaries and Christian workers often fail to comprehend what God is doing in the world today because they fail to grasp the nuances of how Jesus was working in the all-too-familiar biblical narrative. As one who has had the unique privilege of being in a position to have an overview of how God is working in unprecedented ways to fulfill his mission to redeem a lost world, I was thrilled to read Bill Jones' book on ministry multiplication. There are others who are both biblical scholars and missiologists, but few would combine these callings and disciplines into the unique leadership of Columbia International University and Crossover Global as did Bill Jones. We have always known we should multiply witnesses and multiply disciples but have failed to see that this is only a part of the equation. That multiplication of extended witness to the nations was, indeed, the ultimate objective of Jesus' call to follow him and his life-on-life mentoring of the twelve. This book will inspire you to emulate that pattern."

—JERRY RANKIN
President Emeritus, International Mission Board,
Southern Baptist Convention

"In times of tectonic change and a ripening global harvest, Bill Jones unpacks an enduring biblical paradigm for how we should view our mission—and how you can impact the world!"

—STEVE RICHARDSON
President, Pioneers-USA

"*The Ministry Multiplication Cycle* was introduced to me when I was one of Dr. Jones' students nearly twenty years ago. Today, after using its principles on three continents, I can confidently say this book is a must-read for church planters around the globe. Dr. Jones is a gifted missions strategist who practices what he teaches."

—BRENT MCHUGH
Director, Christar International Network

"The ministry multiplication cycle class that I took twenty years ago under Dr. Bill Jones was a turning point in my missional education. It has been not only my personal philosophy of ministry since then, but also the core of my teaching curriculum across the French-speaking world. The concept is thoroughly biblical, theological, missiological, and practical. I am deeply thankful that his teaching is now available in book format. A must-read for every reflective practitioner!"

—RAPHAEL ANZENBERGER
President, Global Evangelists Forum

"The challenge presented in the book is as big as the world. It has to be accomplished among different cultures, languages, histories, and ethnicities. Bill has researched and prepared a theologically sound, practical, and culturally sensitive book to enable church planters to present the gospel and plant churches. The book expresses twenty-five years of leading a ministry that has planted over two thousand churches among unreached people groups. Bill has highlighted the eternal biblical principles and in his missionary experience in a brilliant way has 'seen Eastern Europeans plant churches in Central Asia and the Central Asians reached then plant churches in China.' The future has arrived! Formerly unreached groups are now taking an active role in fulfilling the Great Commission."

—ROBERTO SILVADO
Vice President, Baptist World Alliance

"Simple. Memorable. Practical. Profound. These words describe the steps by which Bill Jones guides us from a fresh framing of the story of Jesus to the multiplication of disciples and churches both locally and cross-culturally. With refreshing candor, warmth, and humor he recounts his own journey of lifelong discovery, uncovering timeless principles to guide fruitful ministry in every context."

—DAVID W. BENNETT
Global Associate Director for Collaboration
and Content, Lausanne Movement

"In *The Ministry Multiplication Cycle*, Bill Jones communicates a compelling, practical, biblical strategy for those who desire to be a catalyst for multiplication. This book provides a tested approach—one used by Jesus—that transcends cultures for the purpose of fulfilling the Great Commission. I hope you will read this book and more importantly, implement its steps."

—FRANK HARRISON
Chairman and CEO, Coca Cola Consolidated;
Founder, With Open Eyes

What Church Planters Are Saying

"Those that know Bill Jones will immediately recognize his 'voice' in this book. If you close your eyes for a moment you can hear the evangelist speaking urgency. As you read the book you will see the process thinker he is. For me, the shining values of the book are Bill's passion for lost people everywhere; his strong commitment to the understanding, explanation, and obedience to the Bible; and the systematic way he develops his ideas. I hope that the many who read his book will also pick up the grand opportunity of our day, to see the prayers of generations of Jesus' servants from all over the world fulfilled: world evangelization and the return of our Lord!"

—DWIGHT SMITH
Founder, Saturation Church Planting International
and the Global Fellowship

"Several books have been published on the topic of multiplication over the past few years. It is trendy to write about this topic. You may even be feeling multiplication-fatigue. However, before writing off this matter and moving on: Stop! Read this book! In a unique way, Jones takes readers on a journey to understand biblical principles and consider contextualized practices related to multiplication strategy. The ministry multiplication cycle advocated here is simple, solid, and highly reproducible among the peoples of this world. As a mission leader, Jones develops this material from a quarter-of-a-century of experience in forty countries and among seventy unreached people groups. He knows what he is talking about! We would be wise to listen and learn!"

—J. D. PAYNE
Author of *Discovering Church Planting*
and *Missional House Churches*

"As a church planter and ministry leader in Azerbaijan we had the desire to extend the kingdom of God by planting sustainable churches, but we did not really know what to do. This book answered our questions. We learned how to evangelize in our own cultural context, how to establish new believers, how to equip church leaders, and how to send people to multiply new church plants. We applied every step in this book and we have seen the results with almost 150 new churches planted."

—IDRIS MAMMADOV
Founder and Director,
ALOV Church Planting Network, Azerbaijan

"I met Bill for the first time many years ago in a gathering of ministers from Central Asia and the Middle East. I was very impressed by his knowledge of Jesus' way of raising the Twelve to be world-changers. When I heard that he was writing this book, I celebrated. I had been waiting for it. Bill addresses an issue that we as pastors, leaders, missionaries, and teachers of the word have been searching and praying to discover: the secret of Jesus' success. If you are desiring to find out how Jesus trained his disciples, this book is exactly for you."

—ALI KALKANDELEN
President, Turkish Protestant Churches Association

"I am very grateful to Dr. Bill Jones because of his books and teaching, which have enabled us to plant 1,280 churches among unreached people groups in India. Because of *The Ministry Multiplication Cycle* we are planting multiplying churches in north India and beyond."

—SOLOMAN GHOSH
Founder and General Secretary, Servants of the
Nations Church Planting Network, India

"The teachings from this book, *The Ministry Multiplication Cycle*, gave our leaders a vision for multiplying new churches among Muslims in every city and village in our country. Now our vision has grown to multiply new churches throughout Central Asia."

—MANSUR ATOEV
Founder and Director,
USHMAH Church Planting Network, Uzbekistan

"Bill Jones is the real deal. I've watched him be fruitful and multiply evangelistically for decades. He has consistently won people to Christ personally, started and grown evangelistic growth ministries, and equipped evangelistic growth church planters globally. This book gives you practical insights into valuable scriptural principles for fulfilling the Great Commission. It will help you prioritize our primary earthly task: making disciples of the unsaved."

—JOHN WORCESTER
President, Church Planting Leadership

"Vintage Bill Jones. Birthed out of the crucible of ministry and biblical studies, Bill offers Gospels-based principles practiced in Acts that work globally when adapted culturally. There's nothing like learning from a self-reflective veteran with a servant's heart. A great read on church multiplication!"

—TOM STEFFEN
Professor of Intercultural Studies, Biola University;
author of *Passing the Baton: Church Planting that Empowers*

"Bill Jones is one of my heroes of the faith—because he embraces the Great Commission and has lived it faithfully for years. This book is deeply biblical and has been field-tested in many countries and contexts around the world. Church planting is the macro-vision that is fleshed out through the micro-strategy of making disciples. Bill links these two concepts together beautifully for the reader and practitioner. I wish I had read this book before planting twenty years ago!"

—JEFF SHIPMAN
Directional Team Member, Christ Together Network

"Dr. Bill Jones introduced me to the ministry multiplication cycle as a student under his leadership many years ago. My takeaway was, and still is, that we are here on the earth for the purpose of multiplying the good news of Jesus around the world. Some fifteen years later, the staff and church planting team of Barefoot Church is still learning from that same message. The ministry multiplication cycle gives us traction as a church family and is our church-wide growth process. If you are seeking to make a difference with your life, I recommend adopting this biblical strategy for multiplication."

—CLAY NESMITH
Senior Pastor, Barefoot Church

What Educators Are Saying

"Dr. Bill Jones is one of the great leaders of twenty-first-century missions and church planting. He has started and led an organization that practically planted many churches. Only heaven will reveal the impact of Dr. Bill Jones' life on the kingdom. As colleague and friend, I wholeheartedly endorse this book and his heart for unreached peoples."

—MARK A. SMITH
President, Columbia International University

"Bill Jones has written an excellent, highly practical, and pragmatic workbook about leading a movement of multiplication. The principles he articulates are applicable to both individuals and churches, forming the basis of a church multiplication movement. I strongly recommend this book not only to church planters, missionaries, and church leaders who wish to develop a multiplication tactical plan, but also to faculty colleagues who teach practical theology to include this book in courses on spiritual formation and discipleship, church planting and multiplication, and Jesus' approach to ministry."

—JUNIAS VENUGOPAL
Associate Dean, School of Mission,
Ministry, and Leadership, Wheaton College

"If the body of Christ is going to fulfill the mandate given to us by the Father and exert massive influence in this unchurched society, it must be intentional in its efforts to multiply itself. Now, more than ever before, it is imperative for the ministries of evangelism and discipleship to push forward by expanding the biblical pathway that will challenge and enrich the kingdom of God. Dr. Bill Jones has provided an epistle that will unleash the plus sign of eternity into our world and communities that will give the twenty-first-century church a practical path for kingdom multiplication."

—JAMES DIXON
President, Antioch Experience
Bible College & Seminary

"It is my great privilege to call Dr. Bill Jones both colleague and friend. As a gifted biblicist with literally decades of preparation in study and practice and the leader of an iconic higher education institution synonymous with the modern missions movement, Bill hones in on the realities and biblical moorings of the why and how that drive the very purpose of missions. *The Ministry Multiplication Cycle* will encourage your heart and challenge your steps as it weaves deep biblical insights with everyday pragmatism."

—PETER W. TEAGUE
President Emeritus, Lancaster Bible College
and Capital Seminary & Graduate School

"Dr. Bill Jones is uniquely gifted as an educator, communicator, and missionary. I have known Bill for several years and this book is the epitome of his commitment to the Great Commission. This distinctive blend paves the way for a biblical missions model that is forward-thinking and especially relevant in today's turbulent times. This book is a must-read for all Christians wanting to maximize their impact for Christ."

—WILLIAM BLOCKER
President, College of Biblical Studies,
Houston and Indianapolis

"Bill Jones possesses an uncanny capacity to confront and confound our tragically self-centered and benign understanding of the Bible's message and methodological assumptions. In *The Ministry Multiplication Cycle*, Jones sets out systematically to deconstruct much of conventional understanding and help the reader to see patterns that most of us simply miss. He demonstrates from incisive scriptural analysis and then illustrates from church history how ministry multiplication is clearly the pattern our Lord modeled and his followers have replicated from the time of the church's birth to the present moment. If you read this book, you will not escape the challenge to get with the master's ministry multiplication program."

—RALPH ENLOW
President, Association for Biblical Higher Education

The Ministry
Multiplication Cycle

The Ministry
Multiplication Cycle

Bill Jones

Foreword by Ken Katayama

WIPF & STOCK · Eugene, Oregon

THE MINISTRY MULTIPLICATION CYCLE

Wipf & Stock
An Imprint of Wipf and Stock Publishers
199 W. 8th Ave., Suite 3
Eugene, OR 97401

www.wipfandstock.com

PAPERBACK ISBN: 978-1-7252-6424-3
HARDCOVER ISBN: 978-1-7252-6425-0
EBOOK ISBN: 978-1-7252-6426-7

Manufactured in the U.S.A.   04/21/20

This book is dedicated to . . .

The students of Columbia International University
who took my classes and studied diligently
to learn Jesus' approach to ministry.

The Crossover Global team who daily implement
the principles of this book in order to plant churches
in some of the most challenging places on earth.

Contents

Foreword

I WAS SURPRISED AND delighted when Dr. Jones asked me to write the foreword for his newest book. He is not only someone that I admire, but also a life-long mentor and friend. I remember clearly the first time I heard the content in this book. It was 1999. I was 19 years old and had recently joined the staff of Crossover Global in Brazil.

As Dr. Jones shared biblical principles with our team throughout the week, my eyes were opened to a reality that would change my way of thinking and doing ministry. Back then, I thought that the Scriptures were only a guide to living a life of obedience that would in turn enable me to honor God. Little did I know that the New Testament was filled with biblical principles for ministry.

In that week, I learned how Jesus taught the Twelve to minister and how the apostles implemented the same biblical principles as seen in the book of Acts. That was both life-changing and ministry-changing.

Fast forward two decades: as I write this forward, I am on a plane headed to Central Asia to teach our 5th generation of potential church planters in the region. I am excited that the very content in training these Muslim background church planters will receive is the same content that you hold in your hands right now!

The Ministry Multiplication Cycle has been the core church planting strategy for Crossover Global. Our entire team has tested and implemented the content of this book in the last 25 years in 37 countries among 71 unreached people groups. The result has been over 2,000 churches planted to date; 62 percent of these churches are second or third generation churches.

What Dr. Jones masterfully unfolds in this book is not a mere set of methodological steps for church multiplication. It additionally serves as the framework for an intentional way of doing ministry. If you are looking for biblical principles for ministry multiplication, this book will become your guide.

It is my prayer that the glorious gospel of Jesus Christ be made known among all peoples of the world through the hands of His global Church and for His global glory!

Ken Katayama
President, Crossover Global

Introduction

ONE WINTER AFTERNOON MY mother called me on the phone. Her voice hinted a bit of concern. A doctor had admitted her to the hospital in order to perform major surgery. She asked if I could come visit her later that day. Since the hospital was located close to my college, it did not take long to make the trip in my grey Chevrolet Nova. I have absolutely no memory as to why my mother was having surgery, but I clearly remember her asking me if she would go to heaven or hell if she died during the surgery.

Why she asked me, of all people, that particular question, I don't know. Perhaps it was because I was going to graduate from college, something she and my dad had not been able to do. More than likely, it was because she had no one else to ask. You see, our family did not go to church on Sundays. Instead, we went water skiing and fishing on a lake outside of Atlanta where we lived. Our extended family didn't really go to church either. A personal relationship with Jesus Christ seemed to have stopped with my grandparents. As a result, addictions, infidelity, divorce, mental health hospitals and suicide left devastating marks throughout the various family structures.

Seeing that the issue of eternity loomed large in my mother's mind, I wanted to get the answer right. I told her that I needed to return to my dorm room to retrieve a little yellow booklet that three of my friends on campus had been reading to me.

It didn't take long before I once again was sitting beside her bed. Opening the yellow tract, I read that God loved her and had a wonderful plan for her life. Her response seems heart-breaking now for she looked at me with a look of amazement and asked, "Really?" I read that she couldn't experience God's love and forgiveness because she had disobeyed God. "I know that," she admitted. As I read, the booklet explained that Jesus Christ died on the cross to forgive her of her disobedience. Again, almost longingly she asked, "Really?" The booklet stated that knowing these truths was not enough to receive God's love and forgiveness. She needed to invite Jesus Christ to come live in her heart. "How do I do that?" she asked. I turned the page and read two words, "Dear God." My mother immediately repeated them after me. Each phrase I read, she repeated, all the way to the "Amen."

Something supernatural took place that afternoon. My mother entered into a personal relationship with Jesus Christ. And He changed her. Something else took place a few weeks after that encounter. I also prayed and invited Jesus Christ into my own heart. And He changed me also!

Within days I was leading other people to Christ. I told everyone I knew or met about God's love and offer of forgiveness. I longed for others to escape the sin and sorrow I had seen in my own family or, even better, to avoid it altogether.

I didn't feel, however, that I was always effective at helping people cross over into a personal relationship with Christ. Sometimes people asked questions I did not know how to answer. Nor did I feel like I was great at helping people grow in their new relationship with Christ. Little wonder. How much can an eighteen-year-old new believer coming from an unchurched, non-Christian, dysfunctional background know? But I did feel that I could get better. That day started a lifelong journey of learning how to be as effective as possible at helping people both come to Christ and grow in Christ.

I started reading everything I thought would help. It wasn't long before I came across a book by Leroy Eims that highlighted the importance of not only leading people to faith in Christ and helping them grow into disciples, but insisted that we need to equip disciple-makers and leaders. His background stressed that without multiplication, we would never reach the world for Christ. That added perspective resonated with me and became a driving force in the ministry God had called me to fulfill.

While I was helping to plant a church in Atlanta, three young female graduates of Columbia International University rocked my ministry paradigm. They politely, but insistently, told me that I did not understand what it took to reach the world for Christ. I explained, perhaps a bit smugly, how if we led people to Christ and discipled them well enough so that they could evangelize and disciple others to do the same, then we would reach the world in our lifetimes.

In the next few minutes, as I listened to these wonderful friends, my whole view of ministry was transformed. Looking back, I am surprised I understood them since they used a lot of unfamiliar words and concepts like cultural boundaries, unreached people groups, cross-cultural communication, and Muslim evangelism. Yet I caught on to what they were saying.

I later heard an analogy that perfectly captured what they were communicating. Until that day, I viewed the world as comprised of 200+ pancakes, or countries. I was convinced that by pouring the syrup of God's love and forgiveness on each pancake, the syrup would spread by virtue of discipleship to the edges of that pancake, or country. Through the patient instruction of my three friends, however, I realized that the world consists, not of 200+ pancakes, but 200+ waffles. As we pour the syrup of the gospel over a waffle (country), it does not spread to the edges of the waffle. Rather, the syrup gets stopped by the waffle squares. These waffle squares represent the 17,000+ people groups found in the over 200 countries. The barriers separating the waffle squares vary, but the most significant barrier is the religious barrier. Other barriers are linguistic, historical and ethnic, or some combination of each. Geography can be a challenge, but not as much in our digital world. For the message of Christ to spread across the waffle, someone (we would call them a missionary) would need to scoop the syrup from one square and carry it over the barrier to another square. Eye opening! So eye opening that after much prayer, I soon made three life-changing decisions.

First, my wife and I, along with a nineteen-year-old named Joao Mordomo, started Crossover Global, an organization that starts churches among people groups (waffle squares) around the world that have little to no access to the message of Christ. Most of our church planters (missionaries) go to Muslim and Hindu cultures. I laugh today at how we naively stepped out in faith and obedience, but God has certainly empowered and blessed our efforts by allowing our missionaries to see thousands of new small churches planted in some of the most difficult places of the world.

Second, I enrolled in a doctoral program at Columbia International University (CIU). Even though I had participated in several mission trips and even spent one semester during college in the Soviet Union, I knew zero about missions. I needed to learn quickly. Since the three young ladies who had opened my eyes to waffles had attended CIU, I figured I should also. Toward the end of my studies (for reasons beyond my understanding), CIU's administration asked me to join the faculty to teach evangelism. I've served there ever since in various roles: professor, vice-president of academics (I hated that position. Honestly!), and president of the university for ten years. Today I serve as the chancellor. (If you have watched Star Wars, you know that Senator Palpatine first became chancellor of the Galactic Republic and later the emperor. Please follow my own career path on social media.)

Third, out of great frustration, I began a study of the ministry of Jesus. Let me explain. More than anything else, I long for people to cross over into a right relationship with Christ. (If I gave it a percentage, I would estimate my longing for people to know Christ would hit around 99%. The other 1% longs for chocolate chip cookies, something about which I feel great shame.) Why did it take me so long to realize that over 40 percent of the world's population not only did not know Christ, but also had no way of ever hearing about Christ because the waffle barriers separated them from having access to the gospel? I considered myself a voracious reader. Why had I not seen a book on world evangelization? I was frustrated that it had taken me years to "get it." I wondered what else I could be missing.

Then it hit me. I had been reading a lot of books about ministry, but I had not gone to *the* book about ministry, the Bible. I was doing what everyone else was suggesting I should do. I began to wonder if I was truly doing what Christ wanted me to do. I figured that if the Bible taught me how to live in a way that pleased Him, then maybe the Bible might also teach me how to minister in a way that would please Him. This thinking launched a two-year, in-depth study of the Gospels to see what I might learn.

The next few chapters of this book share the results of that study from seven different perspectives:

- Chapter 1 provides the foundation for everything that follows by harmonizing the four gospels into one story. The insights gleaned from this process proved invaluable to me and I hope they will for you as well.

- Chapter 2 answers the "so what" question. The material from the first chapter suggests that Jesus emphasized different target groups during different stages of His ministry. It appears He is following a clearly laid out strategy of ministry.

- Assuming that He did follow a strategy, chapter 3 provides ten practical steps, which add some flesh to Jesus' tactics.

- Chapter 4 is critical. If Jesus truly was strategic in His to ministry, that is, if Scripture wants to communicate an approach to ministry that is truly timeless, then we should see it replicated by those Jesus trained, the disciples, and those trained by them. So in chapter 4, we examine the book of Acts to verify whether we just might be on to something.

- In chapter 5, we consider if this ministry strategy can be used in cultures other than our own middle-class situations. We North Americans are often guilty of making the claim that our culture-specific programs are what churches need all over the world. As we learn to think in terms of biblical principles, we will see how this ministry of Jesus can be implemented in any culture.

- Chapter 6 shows how differently the ministry of Jesus might look depending on the cultural context of the ministry.

- Finally, chapter 7 looks at the ministry of Jesus from the perspective of where one should start if a person wants to begin implementing Christ's strategy.

Regardless of whether you have just become a follower of Christ or have served as a pastor for decades, you probably have not spent enough time studying *the* book on ministry, the Bible. If you long to become more effective in ministry, let's take a deep dive into Scripture. Let's see what we can learn from Jesus Himself about reaching the world with the good news.

Chapter 1

Historical Perspective

What Did the Ministry of Jesus Look Like?

IF YOU ARE LIKE most followers of Christ who want to impact the world for His glory, you are very busy. Just taking the time to read a book like this may seem like a luxury. And I suspect that you probably didn't read the previous introduction—you wanted to get right to the heart of the book, glean what can make you more effective at your ministry, and move on.

But wait! You need to read the introduction to this book. It won't take you three minutes. It will, however, help you know where we are going. Realizing the destination will motivate you to finish this critical chapter. Though perhaps not very exciting at times, this chapter is absolutely necessary because the information forms the foundation for everything that follows. So be quick about it. Go back and read the introduction.

Welcome back. Let's get started.

The Story of the Bible

I'm convinced that the average Christian doesn't know the Bible very well. Worse, I'm convinced that the average Christian worker doesn't know the Bible very well. Even worse, the average pastor doesn't know the Bible very well. Sure, most know *stories from* the Bible, but do they really know the *story of* the Bible? This concern motivated me to write two books, *Putting Together the Puzzle of the Old Testament* and *Putting Together the Puzzle of the New Testament*. Both simply and memorably seek to communicate the unifying story of Scripture. Together these books divide the Bible into ten historical eras. To help remember these ten eras, I organized them into five pairs of opposite words:

Nothing/Something

Exiting/Entering

United/Divided

Scattered/Gathered

Coming/Going

Elaborated, the Old Testament part of the story goes like this:

- God creates the human race out of *nothing*. (Genesis 1–11)

- He turns the Hebrew race into *something*–a people of great size and significance. (Genesis 12–50)

- Next we find the Hebrews *exiting* Egypt, but wandering forty years in the wilderness because of unbelief. (Exodus to Deuteronomy)

- Then we see the Hebrews *entering* the Promised Land, experiencing physical victories and spiritual defeats. (Joshua to Ruth)

- Three kings rule over the twelve Hebrew tribes in a *united* kingdom called Israel. (I Samuel to I Kings 11, plus the poetry books)

- Israel is *divided* into two nations, Israel and Judah. Assyria later conquers Israel. (I Kings 12 to II Kings 23, plus several books of the prophets)

- Due to disobedience, Judah is *scattered* when Babylon takes them into captivity. (II Kings 24–25, plus Daniel and Ezekiel)

- Judah is *gathered* back to the Promised Land after seventy years of exile in Babylon. (Ezra to Esther, plus the last three books of the prophets)

Four centuries after Malachi writes the final book of the Old Testament, the promised Messiah is born and the New Testament begins. Two eras complete the *story of* the Bible:

- Old Testament prophecy is fulfilled with the *coming* of Christ. (Matthew to John)

- Before ascending into heaven, the resurrected Jesus commissions the *going* of the Church. (Acts to Revelation)

This information is fairly simple, yet seldom understood. That's not surprising. The Bible is a very thick book. At least we know the story of Jesus very well.

Or do we? How well do we really know the ministry of Jesus? Let's take an easy test and find out.

Question: How long did Jesus minister with the twelve disciples? Commit yourself by writing your answer below.

If you wrote three years as most do, you are wrong. (Ouch!) If you were a bit more technical and wrote approximately three and a half years, sorry, but you are still wrong. Until I stepped away from books on ministry and spent time in the Bible investigating the ministry of Jesus, I would have written the same as you. Why? Because that's what we have been taught since Vacation Bible School. But that's not what the Bible says. Before you throw this book in the trash and label me a heretic, let's look at Scripture. Mark 3:13–19 says,

> And He (Jesus) went up on the mountain and summoned those whom He Himself wanted, and they came to Him. And He appointed twelve, so that they would be with Him and that He could send them out to preach, and to have authority to cast out the demons. And He appointed the twelve: Simon (to whom He gave the name Peter), and James, the son of Zebedee, and John the brother of James (to them He gave the name Boanerges, which means, "Sons of Thunder"); and Andrew, and Philip, and Bartholomew, and Matthew, and Thomas, and James the son of Alphaeus, and Thaddaeus, and Simon the Zealot; and Judas Iscariot, who betrayed Him.

As we read our Bibles and get to this passage, we subconsciously think that since the twelve disciples were always with Jesus, then this event marks the beginning of Jesus' ministry. But does it?

Interestingly, this passage in chapter 3 is not the first time we read in the Gospel of Mark about Peter, Andrew, James, John or Matthew. For some reason, however, by the time we get to Mark 3 and the story of Jesus choosing the twelve, we have already forgotten about earlier experiences Jesus had with some of His disciples. Take Mark 1:16–20, two chapters earlier, for example. That passage says,

> As He (Jesus) was going along by the Sea of Galilee, He saw Simon and Andrew, the brother of Simon, casting a net in the sea; for they were fishermen. And Jesus said to them, "Follow Me, and I will make you become fishers of men." Immediately they left their nets and followed Him. Going on a little farther, He saw James the son of Zebedee, and John his brother, who were also in the boat

mending the nets. Immediately He called them; and they left their father Zebedee in the boat with the hired servants, and went away to follow Him.

Did you catch that? Jesus had a significant relationship with Peter, Andrew, James and John two chapters (and several months) before He called them to be part of the Twelve.

I heard a couple of speakers suggest that it was in Mark 1:16–20 that the ministry of Jesus began. They described the events leading up to Jesus' calling of the four accurately enough, but unfortunately came to a wrong conclusion. They highlighted the ministry of John the Baptist (1:1–8), the baptism of Jesus (1:9–11), the temptation of Jesus in the wilderness (1:12–13) and Jesus' move to Galilee after John's imprisonment (1:14–15). They then reached the story of Jesus calling Peter, Andrew, James and John (1:16–20), which is the first time Mark has mentioned anything about any of the disciples. The speakers then confidently (but inaccurately) declared that as Jesus the Messiah approached the fishermen, the powerful spirituality radiating from the Messiah overwhelmed the four fishermen so much that when He called them, all four left their professions and followed a total stranger. Thus began the ministry of Jesus.

But Jesus did not meet Peter, Andrew, James and John for the first time in Mark 1. He met them much earlier. Most people don't realize that Mark wants to focus on Jesus' ministry in the northern district of Galilee. He doesn't spend much time on what Jesus did early in His ministry in the southern district of Judea. It's not that Jesus' first year of ministry was unimportant. It is just that Mark is in a great hurry to discuss Jesus' ministry in Galilee. As a result, he skips an entire year in the life of Jesus: everything that occurred between Jesus' wilderness experience (Mark 1:13) and Jesus' move to Galilee (Mark 1:14). (Luke does the exact same thing between Luke 4:13 and 4:14.)

Let me repeat. Between two verses of Scripture, Mark and Luke skip a year in the ministry of Jesus.

What then happens during this "missing" year? One must turn to the Gospel of John to find the answer. In John 1:29 we find

Jesus returning from His wilderness experience. (Note: We know Jesus has already been baptized by the comment John the Baptist makes in John 1:32 about witnessing the Spirit of God descending upon Jesus in the form of a dove. We also previously read in the Gospel of Mark that after His baptism, Jesus immediately went into the wilderness.) In chapter 1 of the Gospel of John, beginning with verse 29, John devotes almost four complete chapters before noting Jesus' permanent move to Galilee in John 4:43. What happens between John 1:29 and 4:43? A lot. But one interesting episode occurs in John 1:35–45. The day after Jesus returns from His fasting and temptation in the wilderness, He meets Andrew, John and Peter (1:35–42). The day after that, Jesus meets Philip and Nathanael (1:43–45). This episode is interesting because it shows that in the first few days after returning from the wilderness, Jesus is interacting with at least five of the future Twelve. In other words, at the beginning of His ministry, during that "missing" year in Mark and Luke, Jesus begins to minister *to* His future Twelve.

So back to our little quiz at the beginning of this chapter. If we had asked the question, "How long did Jesus minister *to* the Twelve?" we could have correctly answered three to three and a half years by referring to John 1:35–45. But we asked the question, "How long did Jesus minister *with* the Twelve?" That is, how long did the Twelve travel as a group around the clock with Jesus? From Mark 3:13–19, we now see that we must answer around one and a half years. (Prepositions are important!)

Please understand, our intention is not to make a big deal about the actual starting date of Jesus' ministry. What we are trying to do is show how little we truly understand about the ministry of Jesus. A lot happened in His ministry before He called the Twelve to be *with* Him on a permanent basis. As a result, the question we must then ask is, "What was Jesus doing during this time?" Up until now, we have worked backwards chronologically just to make the point that we don't know as much about the ministry of Jesus as we thought we did. For the remainder of the chapter, we will trace in chronological order the ministry of Jesus from its beginning to its end. Once we finish, we will see in the next chapter what we can learn to make us more effective in our own ministries.

The Ministry of Jesus

Tracing chronologically the ministry of Jesus requires that we first harmonize the gospel accounts by merging the four separate stories—Matthew, Mark, Luke, and John—into one seamless narrative. Two basic approaches exist for harmonizing the gospels. One is quite involved but very rewarding; the other is relatively easy, but still very rewarding.

The first approach requires that we identify all the historical markers in the four gospels such as references to the reign of Augustus Caesar or the administration of Pilate, as well as the various Jewish feasts mentioned in the Gospels like the feasts of Passover, Tabernacles and Dedication. Using the years from the historical markers and the months of the year from the Jewish feasts, we can develop a basic framework for when the various passages occur. For example, we know that a Passover (such as in John 2:13 or John 6:4) occurs around March to April and that the Feast of Dedication (such as in 10:22) occurs around December. Once you have established this basic framework, you can determine the timing of many of the passages, but not all of them. For the remaining passages you will need to spend many hours studying several reference books as you decide where to place them. If diligent, you should finish your harmony after several intense months. It took me almost two years, but I had a job that required that I go to work every day. If you invest significant time and a great deal of effort into this approach, the results are quite rewarding because you will know the ministry of Jesus and your Bible much better.

The second approach does not require nearly the effort. Go online and purchase a reputable harmony of the gospels. I recommend Robert L. Thomas and Stanley N. Gundry's *A Harmony of the Gospels*. This approach is also rewarding; it saves you much time because others have spent lifetimes seeking to develop a credible timeline.

In Appendix A you will find a detailed harmony of the Gospels. Scholars may disagree on some of the finer points, but it suffices for what we want to accomplish. In the following pages, however, you will find a simplified harmony of the gospels, with the life of Jesus divided into four periods: Christ's Private Period (from His birth to the beginning of His public ministry), Christ's Public Period (starting after His temptation in the wilderness and finishing at the beginning of His Passion week), Christ's Trials Period (starting Palm Sunday and ending the following Saturday), and Christ's Triumphant Period (starting at His resurrection and ending at His ascension). Christ's Private Period consists of seven groups of people; His Public Period covers seven geographical locations; His Trials Period lasts for seven days; and His Triumphant Period highlights three confidence boosters. I have summarized these four periods in four charts. Please note that I prefer an AD 30 date for the crucifixion. If you prefer an AD 33 crucifixion date, just add three years to the dates in Charts II, III and IV. Also note that Matthew tends to arrange his content topically, rather than chronologically, making it seem a bit confusing when compared to the other authors.

The Private Period of Christ begins with His birth to *Mary and Joseph*, immediately followed by the *angels and shepherds* offering Him worship. Six weeks later, in obedience to the Mosaic law found in Leviticus 12, Mary and Joseph take Jesus to the temple in Jerusalem. There *Simeon and Anna* honor baby Jesus. Luke 2:39 tells us that after Mary and Joseph "performed everything according to the Law of the Lord, they returned to Galilee, to their own city of Nazareth." Apparently they later return to Bethlehem, perhaps to be closer to the temple, but soon Jesus is sought by the *Magi and Herod*. The wise men want to worship Jesus and Herod wants to kill Him. As a young boy, Jesus interacts with the *temple teachers*. Years later, as Jesus prepares to start His public ministry, He is baptized by *John the Baptist* and then tempted for forty days by *the devil* in the wilderness. See Chart I for the details.

Chart I: The Private Period of Jesus Christ (Seven Groups of People)

When	Where	What	Matthew	Mark	Luke	John
Approx. 6–4 BC	Bethlehem	Born to Mary and Joseph	1:1–25		1:1— 2:7	1:1–18
Approx. 6–4 BC	Bethlehem	Worshiped by the Angels and Shepherds			2:8–20	
Six weeks later	Jerusalem	Honored by Simeon and Anna			2:21– 40	
Approx. two years later	Bethlehem, assuming they re-turned from Nazareth	Sought by the Magi and Herod	2:1–23			
Around AD 6–8	Jerusalem	Taught by the Temple Teachers			2:41– 52	
Late AD 26	Jordan River	Baptized by John	3:1–17	1:1–11	3:1–22	
Late AD 26	Wilderness	Tempted by the Devil	4:1–11	1:12–13	4:1–13	

The Public Period of Christ focuses on His three to three-and-a-half-year ministry. To keep all that happens in order, we arrange the events according to the main geographical areas where Jesus spends the majority of His time ministering. Many times the Lord may travel outside of the stated area, but these tend to be short trips. For example, in John chapter 2, Jesus travels from Judea to Cana in Galilee for the wedding, but soon returns to Judea. To give context, the following map shows the five districts of Palestine during the time of Jesus. The districts of Judea, Samaria and Galilee tend to be more familiar to us than the districts of Decapolis (a mostly Gentile area) and Perea, the district the gospels tend to refer to as "beyond the Jordan."

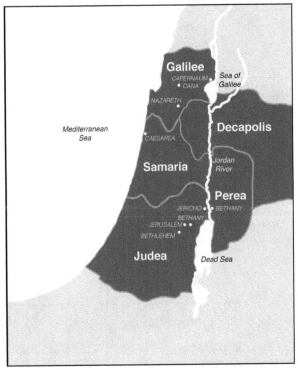

The Five Districts of Palestine during the New Testament

Jesus begins His Public Period based primarily in the district of Judea. Since He will later return to Judea at the end of the Public Period, we will call this part of Jesus' ministry His *Early Judean Ministry*. During this time, we read of Him meeting five of the future twelve disciples (John 1:35–51), going to the wedding in Cana where He turns water into wine (John 2:1–12), cleansing the temple for the first time (John 2:13–25), interacting with Nicodemus (John 3:1–21), and spending time with His disciples baptizing (John 3:22).

After Herod takes John the Baptist into custody, Jesus leaves Judea and travels through Samaria where He meets the woman at the well. Though His *Samaritan* Ministry lasts for only a few days, it is very significant in that many Samaritans (a people who were part Jewish and part Gentile) come to Jesus as their Savior (John 4:42). As Jesus moves into the district of Galilee, we find Him finishing His first year of public ministry. (Here's something to think about, but only for a moment. In John 4, as Jesus talks to the woman at the well, John mentions that Jesus has disciples traveling with Him (John 4:8). Who are they? Be careful now. You must remember that Jesus has not yet called the Twelve to be with Him on a full-time basis. Remember, too, that future disciples like Peter and Andrew live in Capernaum in Galilee, where they work as fishermen. On the other hand, we must also wonder if John is perhaps writing about the time with the Samaritans as an eye witness. We will return to this thought later.)

Jesus spends the majority of His public ministry in Galilee, so the gospel writers devote many chapters to this time frame of His ministry. They write so much about Jesus' time in Galilee, that it helps to divide this aspect of His ministry into three parts. During the initial part of Christ's time in Galilee, what we will call the *Early Galilean Ministry*, among other things Jesus calls Peter, Andrew, James and John to leave their nets and follow Him (Mark 1:14–20; Luke 5:1–11). Together they go on a ministry trip throughout all of Galilee where they minister in various synagogues (Mark 1:39–45; Luke 5:12–16). When they return from this trip, Jesus calls Matthew (Levi) to follow Him (Mark 2:13–17; Luke 5:27–32).

A few months later, Jesus calls twelve from among His many followers to minister with Him fulltime. This event, about halfway through His overall ministry, begins what we will call the *Middle Galilean Ministry*. During this portion of Jesus' ministry, He travels with the Twelve from one side of the district of Galilee to the other side. Toward the end, He sends His twelve disciples to minister in teams of two (Mark 6:7–13; Luke 9:1–6).

After a few months, Jesus' Middle Galilean Ministry ends and His *Latter Galilean Ministry* begins when He takes a series of short trips with the twelve disciples to various Gentile areas. During this segment of His ministry, Jesus, along with the Twelve, visits Tyre and Sidon (7:24–30), the district of Decapolis (Mark 7:31—8:10) and Caesarea Philippi (Mark 8:27-38; Luke 9:18-27). After returning to Galilee, Jesus and the Twelve begin the journey south.

As AD 29 draws to a close, Jesus and His ministry team spend a few months in Judea. Apparently, they minister there during the Feast of Tabernacles/Booths (John 7:1—8:59), which occurs around October as well as the Feast of Dedication (John 9:1—10:39) which occurs around December. In the days between these two feasts, Jesus sends seventy of His disciples in teams of two to announce that the Kingdom of God has arrived. We call this time frame the *Latter Judean Ministry*.

In the weeks leading up to Passover and His passion week, Jesus spends His time in the district of Perea, the region Scripture calls "beyond the Jordan." Luke devotes 13:22 to 19:28 of his gospel to these days of Jesus' ministry. We label this part of His ministry the *Perean Ministry*.

Chart II: The Public Period of Jesus Christ (Seven Geographical Locations)

When	Where	What	Matthew	Mark	Luke	John
Late AD 26 to Late AD 27	Early Judean Ministry	See Appendix A				1:19–3:36
Early AD 28	Samaritan Ministry	See Appendix A				4:1–42

When	Where	What	Matthew	Mark	Luke	John
Early AD 28 to around October AD 28	Early Galilean Ministry (arrives in Galilee—appoints the 12)	See Appendix A	4:12–25; 8:2–4, 14–17; 9:1–17; 12:1–21	1:14–3:12	4:14–6:11	4:43–5:47
Around November AD 28 to around April AD 29	Middle Galilean Ministry (appoints the 12—departs for Gentile regions)	See Appendix A	5:1–8:1; 8:5–13, 18, 23–34; 9:18–26; 11:2–30; 12:22–15:20	3:13–7:23	6:12–9:17	6:1–7:1
Around May to September AD 29	Latter Galilean Ministry (arrives in Gentile regions—departs for Judea)	See Appendix A	8:19–22; 15:21–18:35	7:24–9:50	9:18–62	7:2–10
Around October to December AD 29	Latter Judean Ministry	See Appendix A		10:1a	10:1–13:21	7:11–10:39
Around January to March AD 30	Perean Ministry	See Appendix A	19:1–20:34; 26:6–13	10:1b–52	13:22–19:28	10:40–11:54

We identified the final week in the ministry of Jesus as the Trials Period of Christ due to all of His suffering. The gospel writers allocate almost one third of their chapters to these seven days. It does not require much effort to remember the key events that took place on each of these days.

On *Sunday*, having spent the previous night in Bethany at the home of Martha, Mary and Lazarus, Jesus crosses the Mount of Olives into the City of Jerusalem where the people celebrate His Triumphal Entry (Mark 11:1–11; Luke 19:29–44). He returns to Bethany to spend Sunday night.

The following day, *Monday*, Jesus cleanses the Temple by driving out those buying and selling in the temple, as well as overturning the tables of the money changers and the seats of those selling doves (Mark 11:12–18; Luke 19:45–48).

On *Tuesday*, Jesus answers four questions from those seeking to entrap Him and get Him into trouble with the authorities (Mark 11:19—12:44; Luke 20:1—21:6) and two questions from His disciples (Mark 13:1–37; Luke 21:7–38).

Though we cannot be completely confident regarding the exact day, a good case can be made from Luke that Judas plotted with the Pharisees on *Wednesday* to betray Jesus for money (Mark 14:1–2, 10–11; Luke 22:1–6).

Several important events occur on *Thursday*. Jesus hosts what we call the Last Supper with His disciples. Afterward, they walk to a garden on the Mount of Olives where a group from among the chief priests, scribes and elders arrest Jesus. Later, Jesus endures two trials, one with Ananias and the other with the High Priest and the Sanhedrin (Mark 14:12–72; Luke 22:7–65).

On *Friday*, Jesus goes through four more trials: one final religious trial, plus three more civil trials. Pilate presides over the first and third civil trials. Herod Antipas presides over the second one. After the trials, Jesus is taken to the cross where He is crucified and subsequently buried in a tomb cut from rock (Mark 15:1–47; Luke 22:66—23:56a).

On *Saturday*, a group of soldiers is assigned to guard the tomb (Matt 27:62–66).

Chart III: The Trials Period of Jesus Christ (Seven Intense Days)

When	Where	What	Matthew	Mark	Luke	John
Sunday	Jerusalem	Triumphal Entry	21:1–11, 14–17	11:1–11	19:29–44	12:12–19
Monday	Temple	Cleansing of the Temple	21:12–13, 18–19	11:12–18	19:45–48	12:20–50
Tuesday	Temple and Mt. of Olives	Questions & Answers	21:20–25:46	11:19–13:37	20:1—21:38	
Wednesday	Jerusalem	Judas arranges his betrayal (?)	26:1–5, 14–16	14:1–2, 10–11	22:1–6	
Thursday	Jerusalem and Mt. of Olives	Last Supper and Garden of Gethsemane	26:17–75	14:12–72	22:7–65	13:1—18:27
Friday	Jerusalem	Crucifixion	27:1–61	15:1–47	22:66—23:56a	18:28—19:42
Saturday	Jerusalem	Guards placed at the tomb	27:62–66	16:1	23:56b	

The Triumphant Period of Christ's ministry lasts forty days, from His resurrection to His ascension. We can follow and recall chronologically what happens during this period by remembering three confidence boosters. The first confidence booster highlights the *absence of Jesus* from His tomb. Sunday morning visits, first by the women, and later Peter and John, verify that the grave is empty, glorious good news indeed. Yet the initial reaction of the women is the suspicion that the body of Jesus may have been stolen. How could the followers of Christ know He had actually risen from the dead? The next series of events quells their fears and gives them great confidence. Over a span of forty days, the followers of Christ personally see the risen Lord. Scripture records at least *ten appearances of Jesus*. These appearances occur in a variety of locations and groups, from single individuals to large crowds. During the culminating event at the end of the forty days, the followers of Christ watch the *ascension of Jesus* as He is lifted into the air, disappearing behind a cloud.

Chart IV—The Triumphant Period of Jesus Christ (Three Confidence Builders)

When	Where	What	Matthew	Mark	Luke	John
The Absence of Jesus (An Empty Tomb)						
Day 1 (Sunday)	Jerusalem	Verified by the women	28:1–8	16:1–8	24:1–11	20:1
Day 1	Jerusalem	Verified by Peter and John			24:12	20:2–10
The Ten Appearances of Jesus						
Day 1	The tomb	To Mary Magdalene		16:9–11		20:11–18
Day 1	The tomb	To the other women	28:9–15			
Day 1	Jerusalem	To Cleopas and another		16:12–13	24:13–33	

When	Where	What	Matthew	Mark	Luke	John
Day 1	Jerusalem	To Peter			24:34–35	
Day 1	Jerusalem	To the Ten			24:36–43	20:19–25
After 8 days (So either PM of Day 9 or AM of Day 10)	Jerusalem	To the Eleven		16:14		20:26–31
???? (But after a two day walk from Jerusalem)	Sea of Galilee	To the Seven				21:1–25
????	Unknown mountain in Galilee	To the Eleven and maybe to 500 others (1 Cor 15:6)	28:16–20	16:15–18		
????	????	To James (1 Cor 15:7)				
Day 40	Mount of Olives	To the Disciples (Acts 1:6–11, 1 Cor 15:7)			24:44–49	
The Ascension of Jesus						
Day 40	Mount of Olives	Jesus Ascends into Heaven (Acts 1:11)		16:19–20	24:50–53	

Now that we have a simple harmony of the four gospels, we can inspect more closely the ministry of Jesus summarized in Charts II, III and IV. We will take this in depth look in the next chapter.

Chapter 2

Tactical Perspective

*What Can We Conclude about
the Ministry of Jesus?*

IF THE BIBLE TEACHES us what to believe and how to live, doesn't it seem reasonable that it just might teach us how to minister? This question is not suggesting that the Scripture delineates specific methods that are timeless. It would surely be a stretch of the imagination to think that a particular method might transcend the millennia. Philip's chariot-chasing in Acts 8 may have been very effective at reaching Ethiopians with the gospel in the first few years after the resurrection of Christ, but there aren't too many chariots around today. Similarly, how many people two thousand years ago used the internet to reach their family and friends for Christ?

The question does imply, however, that the Scripture just might provide us with ministry principles that are bound neither by time nor culture. In other words, the Bible could give us ministry insights that are not restricted to a first century Jewish/Greek/Roman culture; direction for ministry that is as effective today in the USA (or Central Asia for that matter) as it was two thousand years ago around the Mediterranean Sea.

If the Bible does teach us about effective ministry, then where better to learn these vital skills than from studying the ministry of

Jesus? With that presupposition, let's review for a moment. In the last chapter we gained a simple, yet thorough, overview of the life and ministry of Jesus. We accomplished this feat by harmonizing the books of Matthew, Mark, Luke and John; that is, we arranged the events of the four gospels in chronological order.

We sought to make this overview simple, yet sufficient. We wanted the overview to be simple so we could remember the story of the gospel. We divided the story into four parts. The first, Christ's Private Period, consisted of seven groups of people. The next part, Christ's Public Period, contained seven geographical locations. Christ's Trials Period followed, which we summarized in seven intense days. Finally, Christ's Triumphant Period, gave us three confidence boosters. We sought to make the overview sufficient enough so we could find various events in the gospels. We placed that information in Appendix A in the form of 135 key events. (By the way, you will find numbering these events in all four gospel accounts in the margin of your Bible a very helpful exercise. Remember that none of the gospels contains all 135 events. In my own paper, not digital, Bible, I noted in a different colored ink which events were overlooked by each of the gospel authors. Having that information in front of me as I read helps me keep the story of Jesus in proper context.)

Our ultimate goal, however, is not information, but transformation. While being better informed (translation: having a nice overview of the life and ministry of Jesus) is perhaps a worthy objective in many endeavors, it cannot become our end goal here. Not at all. We must be willing to change anything and everything in our ministries to be more effective at reaching the world for Christ.

But where do we begin? For a quarter of a century, I had the privilege of teaching a course on the ministry of Jesus. Every semester, after three weeks of studying chronologically every episode of Jesus interacting with His followers, I would ask students to break into small groups and collectively identify what they considered to be Christ's major emphases, if any, as He ministered to the people around Him. Additionally, I would ask them to identify the point in His ministry when He seemed to change an emphasis. Once the small groups identified their choices, the class as a whole had to agree on which of the various nominations made the final cut. Year after year, every class but one, identified the same four major emphases in Jesus' ministry. Many years a class might choose one or two additional emphases, but every class, but one, always included the exact same four emphases. (The one class that didn't identify the exact same four major emphases, did identify three of them. And yes, if you are wondering, I was a bit disappointed since they ruined the streak. When I realized that they were going to omit one of the four from their conclusion, I was greatly tempted to manipulate their discussion. Only by remembering that adults learn better via self-discovery than through listening to a monologue was I able to resist the temptation.)

What would you identify as the major emphases in the ministry of Jesus? What follows are the emphases that my classes, as well as many other groups I have taught from various cultural contexts around the world, decided were the most prominent.

Four Emphases

The first emphasis of Jesus' ministry starts at the beginning of His public ministry (at the point when He returns from His forty days of fasting in the wilderness) and ends when He arrives at the Sea of Galilee where He will challenge two sets of brothers to become fishers of men. When asked to summarize this phase of Jesus' ministry, students unanimously concluded that during these first months Jesus stressed evangelism.

Do you agree? To verify, turn to Appendix A, look at events 12 to 23, and then consider the evidence. You can quickly see what Jesus is doing during the first part of His ministry. In addition to turning water into wine, cleansing the temple and moving from Judea to Galilee, Jesus does the following:

- He permits Andrew, John, Peter, Philip and Nathanael to call Him the "Messiah" (John 1:35–51)

- He explains to Nicodemus that he must be "born again" to enter heaven (John 3:1–21)

- He spends time with His followers as He is "baptizing" new ones (John 3:22–36)

- He tells the Samaritan woman that she must ask for living water to experience "eternal life" (John 4:1–38)

- He sees many more Samaritans believe in Him as "the Savior of the world" (John 4:39–42)

- He proclaims in Nazareth that He has come to "preach the gospel" (Matt 4:12a-13; Luke 4:14–30)

During this time frame in the ministry of Jesus, He clearly focuses on outsiders becoming believers. (See Mark 4:10–11, Colossians 4:2–6 and 1 Thessalonians 4:12 for the context of the word "outsider." I prefer this term over words such as "lost" and "unsaved.") During this emphasis, Jesus invites people to receive Him (John 1:12) as the Messiah, the Savior of the world, so they can be born again and have eternal life. Scripture highlights Andrew, John, Peter, Philip and Nathanael as some of those who not only hear but also respond to this wonderful invitation.

It is interesting that during this ministry emphasis, the phrase "come and see" appears prominently. Jesus invites Andrew and John to *come and see* where He is staying (John 1:39). Philip, after proclaiming that he had found Jesus of Nazareth to be the One "of whom Moses in the Law and also the Prophets wrote," tells Nathanael to *come and see* for himself (John 1:44–46). The Samaritan woman, to whom Jesus spoke at the well, tells the men of Sychar to *come and see* the One whom she suspects to be the Christ (John 4:29). The table below summarizes this emphasis.

Four Emphases

Emphasis	Appendix A	When	Focused On	Key People	Key Passage	Key Phrase
Evangelizing	Events 12–23	Early AD 27 to Early AD 28	Outsiders becoming New Believers	Andrew, John, Peter, Philip, Nathanael	John 1:35–51	"Come and see"

Note, however, that once Jesus calls Peter, Andrew, James and John to leave their fishing and follow Him, never again in Scripture do we find Jesus so frequently and personally sharing the gospel. We are not saying that Jesus never again personally evangelizes. Of course, He does. See Mark 2:5 for just one example. It's just that He changes the emphasis of His ministry going forward. He makes a transition, a major transition.

So where do we find the next major emphasis? Students in my classes and groups picked the time frame that begins with Jesus choosing the four fishermen at the Sea of Galilee and ends with Jesus calling the twelve future apostles at the mountain. When questioned as to the focus of this emphasis of Jesus' ministry, students labeled it "discipleship." (We will return to this word "discipleship" in a moment.)

To understand their thinking, refer again to Appendix A, specifically events 24 to 37. As you read the passages associated with these fourteen major events, you find Jesus repeatedly carrying out only a few activities: preaching, teaching, praying, healing the sick, casting out demons, and confronting the Pharisees. Yet He constantly performs these acts of ministry in the presence of His disciples. Although Scripture does not identify by name all of the disciples who watch Him minister during this time, it does name five of them: Peter, Andrew, James, John and Matthew (Levi).

In the first ministry emphasis we found "come and see" to be a key phrase. In this second emphasis of Jesus' ministry, however, we find "follow Me" to be a key phrase. In Mark 1:17 Jesus commands Peter and Andrew to, "Follow Me and I will make you become fishers of men." Later, in Mark 2:14, Jesus also tells Matthew, "Follow Me!"

But wait a second! Jesus had already met at least three of the above five men about one year earlier when He returned from His fasting in the wilderness. Andrew, John, and Peter, at that point during the first (evangelizing) ministry emphasis, placed their faith in Him as the Messiah. Yet now during this second ministry emphasis, we find Jesus calling the trio to follow Him. This challenge to follow Him would seem to make a lot more sense if these three had chosen not to believe in Him earlier, but they had. So what does Jesus mean when He calls Peter, Andrew, James, John, and Matthew to follow Him?

Apparently Jesus is calling these men to a greater commitment of some kind. It seems it is no longer sufficient for them to believe in Him in view of just the benefits. They need to grow in their commitment. It seems that Jesus wants them to follow Him regardless of the consequences. His focus in this ministry phase is on new believers becoming committed followers. It reminds me of the verse, "If anyone wishes to come after Me, let him deny himself, and take up his cross, and follow Me" (Mark 8:34).

Before we move to the next ministry emphasis, let's return to that word "discipleship." Let's use a more specific word than the word "discipleship," since the word discipleship actually summarizes all three of the last ministry emphases (See the Three Phases of Discipleship chart on page 28). The word "establishing" seems to work better. Consider how Paul uses this word in Colossians 2:6–7: "Therefore as you have received Christ Jesus the Lord, so walk in Him, having been firmly rooted and now being built up in Him and *established* in your faith, just as you were instructed and overflowing with gratitude." Look at Romans 1:11, Romans 16:25, Colossians 1:23, and 1 Thessalonians 3:13 for other great verses that show the power of the word "establish." With that in mind, consider the following chart as we summarize the first two emphases.

Four Emphases

Emphasis	Appendix A	When	Focused On	Key People	Key Passage	Key Phrase
Evangelizing	Events 12–23	Early AD 27 to Early AD 28	Outsiders becoming New Believers	Andrew, John, Peter, Philip, Nathanael	John 1:35–51	"Come and see"
Establishing	Events 24–37	Early AD 28 to Late AD 28	New Believers becoming Committed Followers	Peter, Andrew, James, John, Matthew	Mark 1:16–20	"Follow Me"

So what's the third ministry emphasis of Jesus? This ministry emphasis lasts approximately one and a half years–from the time that Jesus calls the Twelve on the mountain until Jesus rises from the grave. The students and various groups alternately labeled this emphasis as either leadership development, ministry multiplication or equipping. Let's examine why.

A brief perusal of events 38 to 122 in Appendix A shows that the gospel writers devote the bulk of their chapters (68 out of 89) to the eighteen months devoted to this third ministry emphasis. During this key block of time, Jesus spends much of His time gathering and establishing more believers as He preaches, teaches, heals and casts out demons. At other times Jesus confronts and rebukes the misguided religious authorities. At all times, however, we find the Twelve constantly at Jesus' side as He develops them both inwardly in terms of their character and prayer life, as well as outwardly in terms of their ministry skills. Within months He has prepared them to a point such that they begin ministering in groups of two. After Christ's ascension, they turn the world upside down.

Jesus' close and constant interaction with the Twelve makes sense in view of the purpose for which He called them. Mark 3:13–15 says, "And He went up on the mountain and summoned those whom He Himself wanted, and they came to Him. And He appointed twelve, so that they would be with Him and that He could send them out to preach, and to have authority to cast out the demons." Who were these chosen ones? Mark 3:16–19 provides a list: "And He appointed the twelve: Simon (to whom He gave the name Peter), and James, the son of Zebedee, and John the brother of James (to them He gave the name Boanerges, which means, "Sons of Thunder"); and Andrew, and Philip, and Bartholomew, and Matthew, and Thomas, and James the son of Alphaeus, and Thaddaeus, and Simon the Zealot; and Judas Iscariot, who betrayed Him."

During this equipping emphasis, Jesus focuses on growing the Twelve from committed followers into effective workers. He does this through on-the-job-training as seen in the key phrase "with Him."

Four Emphases

Emphasis	Appendix A	When	Focused On	Key People	Key Passage	Key Phrase
Evangelizing	Events 12–23	Early AD 27 to Early AD 28	Outsiders becoming New Believers	Andrew, John, Peter, Philip, Nathanael	John 1:35–51	"Come and see"
Establishing	Events 24–37	Early AD 28 to Late AD 28	New Believers becoming Committed Followers	Peter, Andrew, James, John, Matthew	Mark 1:16–20	"Follow Me"

Four Emphases

Emphasis	Appendix A	When	Focused On	Key People	Key Passage	Key Phrase
Equipping	Events 38–122	Late AD 28 to Early AD 30	Committed Followers becoming Effective Workers	The Twelve	Mark 3:14–19	"With Him"

One more emphasis remains. Students identified the final phase of Jesus' ministry as the forty days between His resurrection and His ascension. In their identification of this phase, students tended to describe this emphasis with words such as missions, Great Commission and missions mobilization.

Using events 123 to 135 in Appendix A as reference, you will see that five chapters cover this time frame. Within these verses, Scripture records four times that Jesus communicates a vision for the gospel to be taken to all nations (Matt 28:18–20; Mark 16:15; Luke 24:44–49; John 20:21). If we add the first chapter of the book of Acts, we find a fifth declaration in verse eight. These five declarations of Jesus occur during at least three or at the most four of His ten post-resurrection appearances. The evidence clearly shows Jesus stressing the importance of extending His kingdom to the ends of the earth.

Though other followers of Christ may be in attendance when He makes these proclamations, the Twelve (minus Judas because he is dead) are always in attendance. The only exception to this fact is in John 20:21. Thomas for some reason is absent from the room during this appearance of Jesus and, therefore, did not hear Him say, "As the Father has sent Me, I also send you."

Three Phases Of Discipleship

Came after Him Mark 1:16–20	Co-labored with Him Mark 3:13–19	Commissioned by Him Mark 16:15
Shaped their Values	Shared their Ventures	Sharpened their Vision
Master-oriented	Ministry-oriented	Mission-oriented
Established in their Walk	Equipped for their Witness	Extended to the World
Establishing Phase (Colossians 2:7)	Equipping Phase (Ephesians 4:11–13)	Extending Phase (Acts 13:1–3)
Emphasis on Maturity	Emphasis on Multiplication	Emphasis on Missions
Focused on the Great Commandment	Focused on the Great Commitment	Focused on the Great Commission

Please don't presume that Jesus waited until the last forty days to give His followers a vision for reaching the non-Jewish world with the message of salvation. There is plenty of evidence otherwise. In John 4 the Samaritans of Sychar see Him as the Savior of the world. In Mark 7 the Syrophoenician Gentile woman recognizes Him as the Messiah by addressing Him as the Son of David, a messianic title. In John 12, Philip and Andrew bring Greeks to Jesus. In this last ministry phase, however, Jesus repeatedly emphasizes His heart for all nations. He seems fixated on one priority. He wants His effective workers to become Great Commission Christians, or as some have put it, World Christians.

I struggled with what to call this last emphasis. It makes a lot of sense to call it the mobilization phase or missions phase. But, to be transparent, I eliminated those options for the simple reason that mobilization does not begin with an "E!" (just being honest!). So let's go with extending. The phrase that perhaps best captures this concept of missions, mobilization, extending is found in John 20:21 mentioned above: "I also send you."

Four Emphases

Emphasis	Appendix A	When	Focused On	Key People	Key Passage	Key Phrase
Evangelizing	Events 12–23	Early AD 27 to Early AD 28	Outsiders becoming New Believers	Andrew, John, Peter, Philip, Nathanael	John 1:35–51	"Come and see"
Establishing	Events 24–37	Early AD 28 to Late AD 28	New Believers becoming Committed Followers	Peter, Andrew, James, John, Matthew	Mark 1:16–20	"Follow Me"
Equipping	Events 38–122	Late AD 28 to Early AD 30	Committed Followers becoming Effective Workers	The Twelve	Mark 3:14–19	"With Him"
Extending	Events 123–35	Early AD 30 to Mid AD 30	Effective Workers becoming World Christians	The Eleven	John 20:21	"I also send you"

Five Target Groups

Before we go any further, let's get a clearer understanding of each of the five target groups by developing a biblical definition for an outsider, new believer, committed follower, effective worker and World Christian.

Outsiders

Jesus graphically describes outsiders in John 8:42–47 when He says,

> If God were your Father, you would love Me, for I pro-
> ceeded forth and have come from God, for I have not
> even come on My own initiative, but He sent Me. Why
> do you not understand what I am saying? It is because
> you cannot hear My word. You are of your father the
> devil, and you want to do the desires of your father. He
> was a murderer from the beginning, and does not stand
> in the truth because there is no truth in him. Whenever
> he speaks a lie, he speaks from his own nature, for he is a
> liar and the father of lies. But because I speak the truth,
> you do not believe Me. Which one of you convicts Me of
> sin? If I speak truth, why do you not believe Me? He who
> is of God hears the words of God; for this reason you do
> not hear them, because you are not of God.

Paul adds to the description of outsiders in Ephesians 2:1–3:

> And you were dead in your trespasses and sins, in which
> you formerly walked according to the course of this
> world, according to the prince of the power of the air, of
> the spirit that is now working in the sons of disobedience.
> Among them we too all formerly lived in the lusts of our
> flesh, indulging the desires of the flesh and of the mind,
> and were by nature children of wrath, even as the rest.

These descriptions are listed in the table below:

Outsiders
Do the deeds of their father, the devil
Do not genuinely love Jesus
Do not understand the words of Jesus
Do not believe in Jesus

Outsiders

Are separated from God because of their sin
Walk according to the world
Indulge the desires of their bodies and minds

New Believers

Please understand that when we say "new believer," we do not necessarily mean someone who has recently crossed over into a personal relationship with God. In other words, the adjective "new" does not refer to a certain length of time, but rather to a certain depth of maturity. Unfortunately, Christians do not grow spiritually at the same rate. Some believers may have crossed over ten years ago, but they are still spiritually immature because they have not grown in their relationship with God. Other followers of Christ may have been believers for less than a year but are very mature spiritually. Think 1 Peter 2:2: "Like newborn babies, long for the pure milk of the word, so that by it you may grow in respect to salvation."

The book of First John does a great job of delineating between various levels of spiritual maturity. Consider 1 John 2:12–14 which says,

> I am writing to you, little children, because your sins have been forgiven you for His name's sake. I am writing to you, fathers, because you know Him who has been from the beginning. I am writing to you, young men, because you have overcome the evil one. I have written to you, children, because you know the Father. I have written to you, fathers, because you know Him who has been from the beginning. I have written to you, young men, because you are strong, and the word of God abides in you, and you have overcome the evil one.

In these three verses, John differentiates between three different levels of spiritual maturity: little children, young men and fathers.

When we talk about new believers in this book, we are referring to spiritually immature believers, or as John calls them, "little children." New believers are immature for various reasons. Some have not had the time to grow in spiritual maturity. Others have not taken the time to mature spiritually. A few have not grown much due to disobedience to God in a certain area of their lives.

New Believers

Have been forgiven

Know God superficially

Are spiritually immature

Committed Followers

If a new believer lacks spiritual maturity, it follows that a committed follower of Christ has reached a certain level of maturity in their relationship with Christ. The previous passage characterizes "young men" as spiritually strong, saturated by the Word of God and victorious over the devil. It goes on to describe "fathers" as knowing God intimately. John says that while "little children" may know the Father superficially (verse 13), "fathers" know Him who has been from the beginning (verses 13 and 14). Their understanding of God is deeper, fuller, and far more intimate because the relationship has been tested by time and experience.

Committed Followers

Are spiritually strong

Are saturated by the Word of God

Have learned to overcome the evil one

Have a much deeper understanding of God

Effective Workers

While Scripture defines committed followers in terms of maturity, it tends to describe effective workers in terms of how well they fulfill or accomplish their ministries. You can see this emphasis in the following verses:

- Jesus, Himself, prays in John 17:4, "I glorified You on the earth, having accomplished the work which You have given Me to do."

- Paul proclaims in Acts 20:24, "But I do not consider my life of any account as dear to myself, so that I may finish my course and the ministry which I received from the Lord Jesus, to testify solemnly of the gospel of the grace of God."

- Paul exhorting Archippus writes in Colossians 4:17, "Take heed to the ministry which you have received in the Lord, that you may fulfill it."

- Paul also implores Timothy in II Timothy 4:5, "But you, be sober in all things, endure hardship, do the work of an evangelist, fulfill your ministry."

Many Christians may have ministries, but not all of them accomplish their ministries very well. Effective workers fulfill what God has called them to do.

Fulfill their ministries

World Christians

The Bible defines the last target group in terms of the person's dedication to the task of world evangelization. Note that we used the word evangelization, not evangelism. The latter word represents an activity. The former word stands for a goal. World evangelization is the result of evangelism (plus establishing, equipping and extending). The evangelization of the world will occur when every nation, tribe and tongue has been reached with the message of God's love and forgiveness. When that happens, the church will have completed the Great Commission and the nations will have responded to the message of Christ.

Finishing the task of world evangelization cannot happen without missionary activity. To be a World Christian does not mean that you must become a cross-cultural missionary. It does mean, however, that you have taken personal responsibility for the evangelization of the world. To take personal responsibility for the task of world evangelization is a heart thing, not a head thing. For example, after hearing Jesus repeatedly proclaim the Great Commission, the Twelve understood its importance in their heads. But it took another seven to eight years before they did anything about it. It wasn't until Acts 10–11 that they intentionally began crossing cultural boundaries to reach the Gentiles.

You may be wondering, "How can a person be a World Christian but not be a missionary?" It depends on the role God has called them to fulfill. The task of world evangelization involves people serving in many different roles within several different categories. In Romans 10:13–15 Paul highlights two of the major categories when he writes: "for 'Whoever calls on the name of the Lord will be saved.' How then will they call on Him in whom they have not believed? How will they believe in Him whom they have not heard? And how will they hear without a preacher? How will they preach unless they are sent? Just as it is written, 'How beautiful are the feet of those who bring Good News of good things!'"

In this passage we see that some World Christians are "goers" and some are "senders." A goer may serve in various roles like that of a church planter or a Bible translator. A sender may serve in different roles such as a financial supporter or prayer warrior for those who go. In addition to the categories of goers and senders, you could add mobilizers, trainers and others. Each category has unique roles for people to serve.

The key word that defines a World Christian is "intentionality." Great Commission Christians seek with focused intentionality to reach unreached people groups with the message of Christ.

World Christians

Assume personal responsibility for the evangelization of the world
Fulfill a strategic role such as "goer" or "sender"

In a later chapter we will see that these five biblical profiles help us tremendously in determining where a person is located in terms of his or her walk with God. This information in turn will help us know what we need to do to help the person move to the next level of spiritual maturity.

One Comprehensive Strategy

If you take a close look at the previous summary chart on the four emphases (page 29), especially the first and fourth columns, it seems that Jesus gives us a clear strategy for reaching the nations with the wonderful message of His love and forgiveness. This apparent strategy is comprised of four tactics and five target groups. The four tactics equate to the four emphases: evangelizing, establishing, equipping and extending. The five target groups are the outsiders, new believers, committed followers, effective workers and World Christians.

Putting it all together, a ministry modeled after Christ's ministry would seem to include these four tactics: the evangelizing tactic of moving people from outsiders to new believers; the establishing tactic of growing new believers into committed followers; the equipping tactic of training committed followers to become effective workers; and the extending tactic of transforming effective workers into World Christians.

This apparent strategy makes a lot of sense both biblically and practically. Biblically it makes sense because we see these four tactics on display throughout the New Testament, not just the Gospels. Take the Apostle Paul for example. Ananias first *evangelizes* Paul (Saul) in Acts 9:1–21. The very next verse, Acts 9:22, hints at Paul going through the *establishing* phase as he "kept increasing in strength," moving from a new believer to a committed follower. Five to six years later, in Acts 11:19–26, Barnabas recruits a fully *equipped* Paul to help him do the work of the ministry in Antioch, Syria. After another eight to nine years, Barnabas and Paul leave on their first "missionary" trip in order to *extend* the church to the ends of the earth, seeking to reach every tribe, tongue and nation with the gospel. Though we see this strategy throughout the New Testament, let's continue to emphasize the phrase "an apparent strategy." Before we decisively declare that Christ indeed provides us with a comprehensive strategy for ministry, we need to wait until chapter four. There we will explore the ministries of the people Jesus trained. If they follow the same strategy as Jesus, then we can have great confidence that we have identified a biblical strategy that Christ wants carefully reproduced.

This apparent biblical strategy makes sense practically as well. Consider your own spiritual journey. You probably weren't doing a lot of ministry before you crossed over into a personal relationship with Christ. And it was probably after you came to Christ and started growing in your spiritual walk before you really had much to offer other people in terms of biblical insight. Your own journey points toward these five various stages of spiritual growth.

If we assume for the moment that Jesus has intentionally provided us a strategy for our own ministries, then we would be wise to pay attention. If we want to bring God great glory by presenting Him the nations, we need to follow in His steps. We need to implement the same tactics in our ministries as Jesus did in His ministry.

Two Diagrams

To better conceptualize this ministry strategy, let's put the four tactics and five target groups into a diagram. We will call it the Stair Steps to Spiritual Maturity. This diagram offers several benefits. First, it shows the relationship between all four tactics and five target groups. Additionally, the diagram highlights a fuller understanding of biblical discipleship. Next, it shows how an individual grows in terms of spiritual maturity. Finally, as we shall see later in much more detail, this diagram provides space under each tactic to list the specific ministries used to help someone grow to the next level of spiritual maturity.

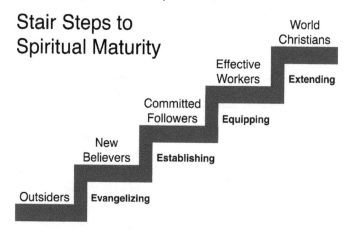

Stair Steps to Spiritual Maturity

Though the Stair Steps diagram has several benefits, it also has some inherent weaknesses. It underscores growing people, but not reaching the world. It provides for various ministries but fails to focus on our ultimate mission. It is more process-oriented than purpose-oriented.

For those reasons and more, let's add a second diagram. Let's call this one the Ministry Multiplication Cycle. Whereas the Stair Steps diagram tends to appear static, the Ministry Multiplication Cycle seems dynamic. It demonstrates how we never finish evangelizing, establishing, equipping or extending. The Ministry Multiplication Cycle displays, well . . . multiplication. It also provides room for ten steps, which we will add in the next chapter. We will find another advantage later since this diagram also allows us to think in terms of reaching different places or locations. Here's another way of putting it: we can follow not only individuals around the cycle, but also entire ministries.

Overall Strategy	Four Tactics
	Evangelizing (John 4:1–42)
	Establishing (Matthew 28:19–20)
Ministry Multiplication Cycle	
	Equipping (Mark 3:14)
	Extending (Luke 24:46–48)

The Ministry Multiplication Cycle

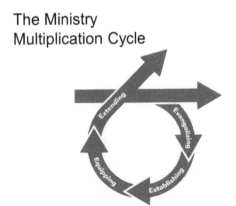

The Ministry Multiplication Cycle does, however, have its disadvantages, one quite glaring. When we look at this diagram, we lose sight of the five target groups.

As we close this chapter, let's take a moment to survey what we have accomplished. By consulting the chronological overview that we developed in the first chapter, we discovered four primary tactics Jesus uses in His ministry. We also found Jesus using these four tactics to impact five different target groups found in Scripture. Thinking we may have discerned an intentional ministry strategy of Jesus, we attempted to capture visually how these tactics and target groups work together to reach the nations with the message of the gospel. This effort resulted in two graphics, the Stair Steps diagram and the Ministry Multiplication Cycle.

Comparison Of Diagrams

The Stair Steps	The Ministry Multiplication Cycle
Growing up	Reaching out
Process	Purpose
Ministries	Mission
Maturity	Multiplication
Target Groups	Tactics
People	Places

In the next chapter we will seek to make this information practical for our individual ministries.

Chapter 3

Practical Perspective

What Basic Steps Does Jesus' Approach
to Ministry Include?

About a year after I crossed over into a personal relationship with Christ, I found myself leading a ministry for Youth for Christ on a high school campus outside of Atlanta. It grew rapidly, no thanks to me–I had no clue what I was doing. I just knew I wanted the students, every single one of them, to become strong followers of Christ.

Intuitively, I knew I would need lots of help in reaching the large campus for Christ. So I recruited three young students in whom I saw great potential. I took these young men to a nearby retreat center where I had stayed many weekends over a four-year period in my earlier search for a right relationship with God. My agenda for the brief retreat was to give the guys a vision for leading their principal, teachers, friends, athletes, band members, honor students, *everyone*, to Jesus Christ.

After checking in with the retreat center's office staff, I immediately got to work. I found a quiet place on the two-thousand-acre property and I cast the vision. But something went shockingly wrong! As I passionately shared my heart with these three young men, I could tell that they weren't grasping what I was saying. The more we talked, the more I realized that two of the students weren't even believers yet.

I quickly switched gears and shared the gospel. Both of the "outsiders" invited Christ into their hearts. They were so grateful that God had forgiven them that they wrestled me to the ground and stuffed hay up my nose. (Teenagers have unique ways of showing their love, don't they?) One of the two eventually became a pastor, and the other a deeply committed Christian businessman.

Great story? From the perspective of Christ changing two young lives for all of eternity, yes. From the perspective of accomplishing the agenda of developing a leadership team to help reach the campus for Christ, absolutely not. Why? Because in my zeal, I completely overlooked several very important steps before trying to recruit these young men to a leadership team. For one thing, if I were considering someone as a potential leader, then I should have certainly known if the person had crossed over into a real relationship with Christ. That's perhaps the most obvious step I missed, but there were other steps I skipped as well.

What are these steps and how do we discover them? We begin by doing a quick review of the key Bible passages associated with the four tactics of the Ministry Multiplication Cycle. Once again, the harmony of the Gospels we developed in chapter one will prove very helpful. As we investigate these passages, we will look for the necessary steps that enable someone to accomplish each tactic effectively. By putting these steps together, we will see clearly how to implement practically the Ministry Multiplication Cycle. Let's begin.

Evangelizing Steps

Recall that during events 12–23 (see Appendix A), Jesus seems to emphasize evangelizing. Three key passages dominate this part of His ministry. In the first passage, John 1:35–51 (event 13), we find Andrew, John (probably), Peter, Philip and Nathanael believing in Jesus as the Messiah, the Lamb of God who takes away the sin of the world. In the next passage, John 3:1–21 (event 17), Jesus tells

Nicodemus that he must be born again. And in the third passage, John 4:1–42 (events 19–20), we read of the woman at the well and her fellow Samaritans receiving the Living Water as the Savior of the world.

Can we delineate any practical steps from these passages? Absolutely. Tucked away between Jesus' conversation with the woman at the well and His outreach to the people of Sychar, we find these verses:

> Jesus said to them, "My food is to do the will of Him who sent Me and to accomplish His work. Do you not say, 'There are yet four months, and then comes the harvest?' Behold, I say to you, lift up your eyes and look on the fields, that they are white for harvest. Already he who reaps is receiving wages and is gathering fruit for life eternal; so that he who sows and he who reaps may rejoice together. For in this case the saying is true, 'One sows and another reaps.' I sent you to reap that for which you have not labored; others have labored and you have entered into their labor." (John 4:34–38)

I love these verses because they provide an inside look at Jesus conducting a seminar with His followers on effective evangelism.

Imagine the situation. Jesus' disciples have just returned from their shopping trip for groceries in the city of Sychar, located about half of a mile away (John 4:8, 27). They arrive just as Jesus finishes His conversation with the woman at the well. The fact that she leaves her water pot at the well indicates that His words must have made an incredible impact on the woman. Perhaps the prospect of personally receiving eternal life (John 4:14) made the woman's negligence unintentional. She could think of nothing else but personal forgiveness, so she forgets the jar. Or, maybe her leaving the water pot was actually intentional. Not having to carry the heavy container would allow her to travel more quickly to tell others that she may have found the Christ. Either way, Jesus apparently impacted her greatly.

With the woman gone, Jesus' followers urge Him to eat. Jesus uses their emphasis on food as a teaching opportunity. He explains that true nourishment comes from doing the will of God and accomplishing His work. To experience real satisfaction, they must realize that they are surrounded by people like the immoral woman who had just left them, people in desperate need of God's forgiveness. A great spiritual crop awaited, one that God wanted harvested. Jesus' followers, however, must do some work. Some need to sow and others need to reap. Over the next two days of ministry, many Samaritans believe that Jesus is the Savior of the world (John 4:39–42).

From these verses we discover Jesus comparing the process of evangelizing outsiders to that of harvesting crops. Harvesting includes three main steps: cultivating the soil, sowing the seed, and reaping the crop

The first step is not specifically mentioned in the above passage, but any farmer or gardener, can attest to the importance of cultivating the soil. My own father grew a large garden in our backyard. When I was a young boy and had to do some of the work, the garden seemed endless. Long before we planted anything, however, we disked and fertilized the soil. There was almost a direct correlation between how well we cultivated and how much we reaped. Sure, other factors were very important, like the amount of rain we received. But simply put, good soil equaled good crops. Just think about the parable of the four soils in Mark 4:3–20.

To bring in a spiritual harvest, we need to follow the same steps. We need to:

1. Cultivate the heart

2. Sow the Gospel

3. Reap the harvest

First, we need to *cultivate* the person's heart through prayer and by building a strong relationship. Some people may require more cultivating than others. Many factors help shape their receptivity to the seed of the gospel. Certainly, God's Holy Spirit superintends everything. From a human perspective, however, the following can make a person more or less receptive:

- age (younger people seem more open to the gospel than older people);

- experiences (people with positive encounters with believers seem more open than those with negative experiences);

- disposition (some people seem more open to different ideas than others);

- struggling in a crisis (people going through trauma seem more open than those who aren't); and

- religious background (people from certain religions seem more receptive than others).

There are also many other factors such as educational level, social status and financial affluence. Who do you think would be the easiest to cultivate: a ten-year-old child who has been raised going to a Bible teaching church by godly parents to hear the gospel, or a thirty five year old Islamic fundamentalist whose family has been persecuted by people who call themselves Christians? The former seems a whole lot easier. God, however, sometimes surprises us. Even though the woman at the well was a Samaritan–a people group that hated the Jews and were in turn a group hated by the Jews–she did not need much cultivating by Jesus. Apparently, the Holy Spirit had been working in her heart. Just keep in mind, that sometimes it may take an extremely long period of time to cultivate a person's heart so that he or she will be able to eventually understand and receive the message of the gospel.

Second, we need to *sow* the gospel. Once the person seems receptive, we need to clearly communicate the message of God's love and forgiveness found in a personal relationship with Jesus Christ. This step may be in a ten minute presentation, or over a period of several years. It seems that Jesus' conversation with the woman at the well took around an hour: about the time it took His followers to walk a half mile to the city, buy food from the market, and walk the return half mile to the well. Regardless of how long it takes, we are seeking to make the plan of salvation clear enough for the person to understand God's offer of eternal life.

The final step of bringing in a spiritual harvest is to *reap* the crop. Once the outsider understands the role that Christ's perfect life, atoning death and amazing resurrection play in providing forgiveness of sin and removal of shame, we need to invite the person to receive Jesus Christ by faith as his personal Lord and Savior. Jesus gave the woman at the well this same offer in John 4:10: "Jesus answered and said to her, 'If you knew the gift of God, and who it is who says to you, "Give me a drink," you would have asked Him, and He would have given you living water.'"

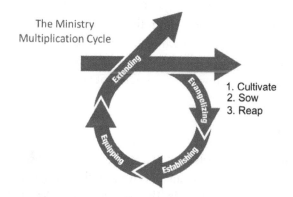

The Ministry Multiplication Cycle

Extending
Evangelizing
Equipping
Establishing

1. Cultivate
2. Sow
3. Reap

By taking the steps of cultivating, sowing and reaping, we fulfill the tactic of evangelizing. We have the joy of helping outsiders become new believers.

Establishing Steps

As seen above, during events 12–23 found in Appendix A, Jesus focuses on evangelizing. In fact, the first chapter of John records the specific circumstances of how five of those who eventually become known as the Twelve cross over into a personal relationship with Christ, moving from outsiders to new believers. As we move into events 24–37, however, we find Jesus taking steps to move five of the Twelve from new believers to committed followers. Here Scripture records our Lord specifically calling Peter, Andrew, James and John (event 24), as well as Matthew (event 31) to a greater level of spiritual commitment.

Keep two things in mind. Remember that Jesus doesn't stop ministering to the crowds while He seeks to establish the future Twelve in a deeper relationship with God. Also remember that by the time Jesus challenges these five men to this greater commitment, at least three of them have been new believers for about one year. Apparently they meet His challenge because a few months later, Jesus will call them to be part of His inner circle.

Does a passage exist that would help us clearly understand the steps associated with the establishing tactic? Yes, a very famous one, Matthew 28:19–20. It says, "Go therefore and make disciples of all nations, baptizing them in the name of the Father and the Son and the Holy Spirit, teaching them to observe all that I commanded you; and lo, I am with you always, even to the end of the age." This passage provides two simple, but powerful steps:

4. Baptize

5. Teach

First, Jesus exhorts us that after we go and tell people about the message of God's love and forgiveness, that we should *baptize* those who respond positively. The point here is not how to baptize a person, or who should do the baptizing, or at what age the person should be who gets baptized. This passage simply directs us to add the step of baptism.

Second, to help move a person up the spiritual stair steps from a new believer to that of a committed follower, we need to *teach* the person to obey all that Christ has commanded us. Note, the step involves much more than a person simply knowing what he or she should do. This fifth step expects obedience to the truth. We could define it like this:

Biblical Teaching = Information for the Head + Transformation of the Heart + Application from the Hands

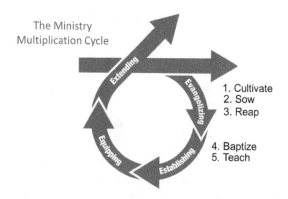

The Ministry
Multiplication Cycle

Extending
Evangelizing
Equipping
Establishing

1. Cultivate
2. Sow
3. Reap

4. Baptize
5. Teach

Whereas we might baptize someone in a matter of seconds, teaching a new believer to obey everything that Christ has commanded may take months, even years, depending on the situation. Our goal, however, is not simply to explain the Bible, but to establish the believer. But we aren't finished yet.

Equipping Steps

We now come to events 38–122 during which Jesus focuses on equipping the Twelve so that they become effective workers for the Kingdom. At this point in the gospel story, Scripture mentions all twelve of the apostles by name at least once. A few of them (like Andrew, Philip, Matthew, Thomas and Judas) appear multiple times. Three in particular (Peter, James and John) are mentioned repeatedly.

What steps does Jesus take to equip the Twelve? Mark 3:14–15 gives a great summary: "And He went up on the mountain and summoned those whom He Himself wanted, and they came to Him. And He appointed twelve, so that they would be with Him and that He could send them out to preach, and to have authority to cast out the demons." Breaking the passage into its components allows us to see the three steps Jesus follows to turn the Twelve into effective workers.

6. Select potential workers—"Summoned those whom He Himself wanted . . . He appointed twelve"

7. Prepare emerging workers—"So that they would be with Him"

8. Mobilize developed workers—"That He could send them out to preach . . ."

The first equipping step involves *selecting* the potential workers. By this point in the ministry of Jesus, He has large crowds following Him. From passages like the feeding of the five thousand (Mark 6) and the feeding of the four thousand (Mark 8), we can have some idea of the size of the multitudes that surrounded Him. From the multitudes, Jesus chooses only twelve. This decision had to have been very important since the future of His mission rested upon their success going forward. With that in mind, it is very interesting that Luke 6:12–16 informs us that Jesus spent the entire night in prayer prior to calling the Twelve.

In the second equipping step, *preparing* the emerging worker for effective service, Jesus preferred "showing" the Twelve over "telling" the Twelve how to minister to others. To that end, Jesus rarely did anything without these men watching and listening. Many times Scripture speaks of Jesus debriefing with the Twelve after a ministry experience, whether it meant answering questions about how to cast out demons or explaining why someone healed of blindness might have been born that way. The fact that they could observe Jesus preaching, teaching, praying and serving, made an indelible impression on them. Scripture speaks of their later recalling these things to mind long after Jesus was gone. Jesus' training of these men was constant, close and concrete. It was not limited to Sunday mornings from behind a pulpit discussed in the abstract.

At a certain point the Twelve were prepared, or at least as much as one can be prepared. The time had come for Jesus to send them out to do what He had been equipping them to do. It was time for the third and final step, *mobilizing* the newly developed leaders. They were ready for Jesus to send them to minister on their own.

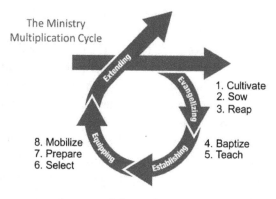

The Ministry
Multiplication Cycle

1. Cultivate
2. Sow
3. Reap

8. Mobilize
7. Prepare
6. Select

4. Baptize
5. Teach

The moment Jesus mobilizes the Twelve, something very powerful occurs: multiplication takes place. As the Twelve take others through the same process that Jesus took them, huge numbers of workers are produced, numbers that ultimately would become large enough to reach the nations with the message of Christ, if it were not for one problem: cultural barriers. Two more steps are needed for the message of the gospel to reach every man, woman, boy and girl.

Extending Steps

After His resurrection, Jesus begins moving the Twelve, except for Judas who has recently died, from the spiritual stair step of effective worker to that of a World Christian. Scripture mentions several of the Twelve by name during this emphasis: Peter, Thomas, Nathanael, James and John.

This final set of events, numbers 123–135 in Appendix A, cover only forty days. Yet during this time Jesus repeatedly focuses on spreading the message of the Gospel to all *ethne*, or ethnolinguistic groups. Christ desires representatives from every people group, what we described in the introduction as waffle squares. If you count Acts 1:8, Scripture records five different times when the Lord mandates that the Twelve cross cultural boundaries in order to take the Gospel not only to the Jews, but also to the Samaritans, and ultimately to the Gentiles. He wanted everyone to have the opportunity to enter eternal life.

What steps does Jesus take to extend the Twelve to every tongue, tribe and nation? Luke 24:46–48 gives us tremendous insight. In these verses, Jesus says, "Thus it is written, that the Christ would suffer and rise again from the dead the third day, and that repentance for forgiveness of sins should be proclaimed in His name to all the nations, beginning from Jerusalem. You are witnesses of these things." We have two steps from these verses that help move effective workers to World Christians. Just like Jesus, we need to:

9. Challenge workers—"forgiveness of sins should be proclaimed in His name to all the nations"

10. Send workers—"You are witnesses of these things"

In the first extending step Christ *challenges* the Twelve with a vision for the world, for reaching every nation. Do not lose sight of the fact that when they heard the word "nations," they did not think of geo-political entities. Rather, they thought of ethno-linguistic groups. They thought of cultures, not countries. Nations did not exist in Bible-times like they do today. So over the forty days of His resurrected ministry, Christ stresses over and over again a vision of crossing cultural barriers. See these examples in Scripture:

- Matthew 28:19: "Go therefore and make disciples of *all the nations*"

- Mark 16:15: "Go into *all the world* and preach the gospel to all creation."

- Luke 24:47–48: "forgiveness of sins should be proclaimed in His name to *all the nations* . . You are witnesses"

- Acts 1:8: "you shall be My witnesses . . . even to *the remotest part of the earth*"

But for the nations to be reached with the message of God's love and forgiveness in Christ, someone has to take the gospel. Someone must *go* to the various unreached people groups. Romans 10:13–15 quickly gets to the heart of the matter when Paul writes, "for 'whoever will call on the name of the Lord will be saved.' How then will they call on Him in whom they have not believed? How will they believe in Him whom they have not heard? And how will they hear without a preacher? How will they preach unless they are sent? Just as it is written, 'How beautiful are the feet of those who bring good news of good things!'"

It follows that in the second extending step, Christ *sends* the apostles to fulfill this glorious task. Consider the previous verses once again, but from the perspective of this second extending step:

- Matthew 28:19: "*Go* therefore and make disciples of all the nations"

- Mark 16:15: "*Go* into all the world and preach the gospel to all creation."

- Luke 24:47–48: "forgiveness of sins should be proclaimed in His name to all the nations . . . *You are witnesses*"

- Acts 1:8 "*you shall be My witnesses* . . . even to the remotest part of the earth"

Is Scripture mandating that every one of His followers leave his home culture and serve as a missionary in some far away culture? Look back at Romans 10:15 when it asks, "How will they preach unless they are sent?" For goers to go, they must be sent. For the church to fulfill the task of world evangelization, we need goers *and* senders. What makes someone a World Christian is not their position, but their motivation. A World Christian is someone who has taken personal responsibility for reaching the unreached people groups of the world. The actual role that he or she plays is secondary. The following chart shows how these ten steps relate to the four tactics and the overall strategy of Jesus.

Overall Strategy	Four Tactics	Ten Steps
		Cultivate
	Evangelizing (John 4:1–42)	Sow
		Reap
	Establishing (Matthew 28:19–20)	Baptize
		Teach
Ministry Multiplication Cycle		Select
	Equipping (Mark 3:14)	Prepare
		Mobilize
	Extending (Luke 24:46–48)	Challenge
		Send

Please realize that we are not suggesting that these ten steps are absolute. We just as easily could have identified nine steps, or fifty steps. Our intent has been to give a bit more specificity to the four tactics. We wanted to make the Ministry Multiplication Cycle a bit more practical, so we do not accidentally overlook any important steps as I did during my "leadership" retreat that I mentioned at the beginning of this chapter.

Nor are we suggesting that we must take a new Christian linearly from step four to step ten. In actual ministry, a new Christian may attend a missions conference the day after accepting Christ. While listening to the speaker, he or she may believe God has called him or her to serve as a church planter among a people group in Southeast Asia. This person may seem to be at step nine, ready to go to step ten. But like we said earlier, they would not have much to offer the people of Southeast Asia if they did not complete steps four to eight before their departure. Unfortunately, churches regularly make such unwise decisions. A new Christian may seem motivated and charismatic, so church leadership puts him or her in charge of the youth ministry. These types of decisions invite disaster.

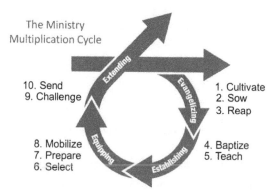

The Ministry
Multiplication Cycle

10. Send
9. Challenge

Extending

Evangelizing

1. Cultivate
2. Sow
3. Reap

8. Mobilize
7. Prepare
6. Select

Equipping

Establishing

4. Baptize
5. Teach

Recall in chapter 1 that we harmonized the four gospels into one unified narrative of the ministry of Jesus. The second chapter showed that Jesus strategically took the Twelve through four emphases, or tactics that moved His followers up the stair steps of spiritual maturity. We gave a name to this apparent biblical strategy, calling it the Ministry Multiplication Cycle. This chapter divided the strategy's four tactics into ten practical steps. These steps help us avoid overlooking important aspects of effective ministry.

Until now we have called the Ministry Multiplication Cycle an "apparent" biblical strategy. In the next chapter, we will explore the ministries of the people Jesus trained. If they follow the same strategy as Jesus, then we can confidently declare that we have identified a biblical strategy that Christ wants us faithfully to follow.

Chapter 4

Biblical Perspective

If the Ministry Multiplication Cycle Is Truly
a Biblical Strategy, Shouldn't We See It
Replicated by Those Jesus Trained?

UP TO THIS POINT, we have resisted calling the Ministry
Multiplication Cycle a biblical strategy. We have thus far tentative-
ly claimed that it "appeared" to be a biblical strategy. To confirm
that we have identified a biblical strategy, we need to move from
the Gospels to the book of Acts and see if the people whom Jesus
trained, the Twelve, replicate the cycle. To add to our confidence,
we would like to see the Ministry Multiplication Cycle reproduced
by the people the Twelve trained.

Two other factors would help convince us of the biblical
nature of the Ministry Multiplication Cycle-the clarity and the
preponderance of the evidence. By clarity, we mean that the four
tactics should be obvious as we trace the ministries of the Twelve
and those whom they trained. We would not need to rely on im-
plications, allusions or speculation. By preponderance, we mean
that the more examples we discover of evangelizing, establishing,
equipping and extending, the more confidence we should have in
our declaration. By adding these criteria together, we set a rather

high bar to meet before we conclude that the Ministry Multiplication Cycle truly is a biblical strategy.

To prepare for our investigation into the book of Acts, it would be helpful to start with a basic overview of this incredible book. Acts 1:8 serves as the organizing verse for the book. In this verse Jesus says, "But you will receive power when the Holy Spirit has come upon you; and you shall be My witnesses both in Jerusalem, and in all Judea and Samaria, and even to the remotest part of the earth." From this verse, we see that God's people will take the gospel from Jerusalem to the world. We can trace the spread of the good news in the book of Acts in a variety of ways. Three specific aspects seem to be quite helpful: geographically, culturally and biographically.

The Five Districts of Palestine during the New Testament

Geographically, the followers of Christ first announce the good news of God's love and forgiveness in the city of Jerusalem

(Acts 2–7), located in the district of Judea. They then travel north to the district of Samaria (Acts 8), eventually reaching the ends of the earth (Acts 9–28). The map on page 75 of the Roman world during the days of the New Testament shows the geographical location of the gospel's advance.

Looking at the book of Acts through a cultural lens adds further insight. The primary culture of the people living in Jerusalem and Judea (Acts 2–7) is Jewish. As you move into Samaria (Acts 8), we find the culture of the people living there to be half Jewish and half Gentile. (Read II Kings 17 for the origin of the Samaritans.) Moving beyond Samaria to the ends of the earth (Acts 9–28), the culture of the people becomes Gentile.

Interestingly, Luke, the author of Acts, seems to emphasize one main character in each of these sections of his book. In Acts 2–7, he highlights Peter who reaches the Jews in Jerusalem and Judea. In Acts 8, Philip becomes the main character as the one who takes the gospel to the Samaritans. Note that this Philip is not one of the twelve apostles (see Acts 8:1), but one of the seven deacons (see Acts 6:5 and 8:5). Finally, Paul takes the stage as he carries the good news to the ends of the earth in Acts 9–28.

Book Of Acts	Chapters 2–7	Chapters 8	Chapters 9–28
Geographical Emphasis	Jerusalem and Judea	Samaria	Ends of the Earth
Cultural Emphasis	Primarily Jewish	Part Jewish, Part Gentile	Primarily Gentile
Biographical Emphasis	Peter	Philip	Paul

We need to consider one other detail before we get started. Who trained Peter, Philip and Paul? We definitely know that Jesus trained Peter. We have spent the last three chapters of this book looking at how Jesus trained him. We also definitely know that

Jesus did NOT train Paul. Paul is known for persecuting followers of Christ until he became a Jesus-follower himself after the resurrected Lord appeared to Him on the road to Damascus. As best as we can tell from a human perspective, Ananias and Barnabas trained Paul. Yet sandwiched between Peter and Paul, we find Philip. Who trained him? We have no clue. Scripture makes no mention of his background. If Philip were part of the 120 people in Acts 1:15, then maybe Jesus trained him. If he were not part of that group, then either one of the Twelve trained him or someone trained by one of the Twelve trained him.

Peter	Philip	Paul
Trained by Jesus	Trained by Jesus or someone else	Trained by someone else

This basic understanding of the book of Acts provides a template for answering our main question: "Did the people who Jesus trained, as well as the people they trained, replicate the Ministry Multiplication Cycle?"

Multiplication of Christians

Let's take a brisk walk through the book of Acts and see if the apostles collectively and Peter, Philip and Paul specifically implemented the four tactics of the Multiplication Cycle. If they indeed practiced evangelizing, establishing, equipping and extending, then we can shred our tentativeness and confidently state that the Ministry Multiplication Cycle is a biblical strategy.

Evangelizing

Let's begin with the apostles in general. Did they practice sowing the gospel and reaping the fruit of people coming to Christ?

Acts 4:33 speaks clearly and persuasively to their evangelistic efforts. It says, "And with great power the apostles were giving testimony to the resurrection of the Lord Jesus, and abundant grace was upon them all." As a result, many people crossed over into a personal relationship with Christ. In addition, Acts 2:43–47 says, "Everyone kept feeling a sense of awe; and many wonders and signs were taking place through the apostles . . . And the Lord was adding to their number day by day those who were being saved." Finally, Acts 5:12–14 adds, "At the hands of the apostles many signs and wonders were taking place among the people; . . . And all the more believers in the Lord, multitudes of men and women, were constantly added to their number." These must have been very exciting times.

Well, what about Peter? Did he personally practice evangelism? Ten days after Jesus ascends into heaven, Acts 2:14–41 tells us that Peter preaches a powerful evangelistic message. In verses 38–40 he proclaims, "Repent, and each of you be baptized in the name of Jesus Christ for the forgiveness of your sins . . . Be saved from this perverse generation!" In response, approximately three thousand people moved up to the second step of the Stair Steps of Spiritual Maturity.

Peter, however, is not done. In Acts 3, Peter, accompanied by John, preaches again that Jesus Christ rose from the dead. Acts 4:1–4 notes,

> As they were speaking to the people, the priests and the captain of the temple guard and the Sadducees came up to them, being greatly disturbed because they were teaching the people and proclaiming in Jesus the resurrection from the dead. And they laid hands on them and put them in jail until the next day, for it was already evening. But many of those who had heard the message believed; and the number of the men came to be about five thousand.

Wonder what it was like to have thousands of new followers of Christ moving about the city of Jerusalem!

Obviously, Peter practiced evangelism, but what about Philip? Acts 8:26–39 communicates the famous story of Philip using a passage from the book of Isaiah to share the good news with an Ethiopian eunuch and leading him to Christ.

Hold on for a moment! If you are tracking with the four tactics of the Ministry Multiplication Cycle, you may be asking, "Since Philip is from Judea and the eunuch is from Ethiopia, why have we designated this encounter as an example of evangelism rather than an example of extending?" Great question. Recall the pancake/waffle illustration from our introduction? (Do you see now why I strongly recommended that you read the introduction? If you haven't read it, now is the time to do it. Things will make a lot more sense.) The tactic of extending focuses on crossing waffle squares, that is, crossing cultural boundaries. Though geography can make sharing the gospel difficult, the real cultural barrier is the religious barrier. From the Jewish perspective, a person was either Jewish or Gentile, with Samaritans being somewhere between the two.

So let's examine Philip and the Ethiopian from a waffle perspective. They both come from different geographical locations, however, they both live within the Roman Empire. They both speak the same language. They both are coming from the same religious affiliation. Remember that the Ethiopian traveled to Jerusalem in order to worship God in the Jewish temple. They both consider Isaiah to be a prophet of God. The only thing that seems to separate them besides a personal relationship with Jesus Christ is where they live. Since very few cultural boundaries are crossed, we use this episode as an example of evangelism. Now, back to Philip's practice of evangelism.

After sharing the good news with the Ethiopian, Philip continues evangelizing. Acts 8 describes him preaching the gospel from Azotus to Caesarea, the seat of the Judean government (v. 40). Along the way, Philip may have proclaimed the gospel in the cities of Lydda and Joppa since they were located on the route from Azotus and Caesarea, all of them near the coast of the Mediterranean Sea. No wonder Luke describes the deacon as "Philip the evangelist" in Acts 21:8.

If Philip carried the moniker of "the evangelist," it would not be unreasonable to tag the Apostle Paul as the "uber-evangelist." He shared the gospel with Jews every place he went: in the synagogues of Damascus when he first came to Christ (9:20–22), during his time in Jerusalem (9:28), in the synagogue of Pisidian Antioch (13:14–43), in the synagogue of Iconium (14:1–5), in Derbe (14:20–21), in the synagogue at Thessalonica (17:1–4), in the synagogue of Berea (17:10–12), with the Jews in the synagogue of Athens (17:17), in the synagogue of Corinth where Crispus, the leader of the synagogue, and all his family believed in Christ (18:4–8), and in the synagogues of Ephesus (19:8–10). He seems to have shared the good news of salvation with every person he met: from a female businesswoman in Philippi named Lydia (16:11–15) to King Agrippa in Caesarea (26:27–29).

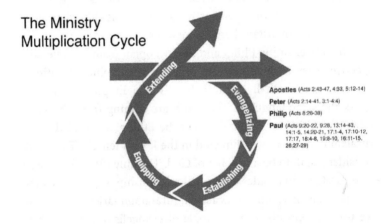

The Ministry Multiplication Cycle

Extending

Evangelizing

Equipping

Establishing

Apostles (Acts 2:43-47, 4:33, 5:12-14)

Peter (Acts 2:14-41, 3:1-4:4)

Philip (Acts 8:26-39)

Paul (Acts 9:20-22, 9:28, 13:14-43, 14:1-5, 14:20-21, 17:1-4, 17:10-12, 17:17, 18:4-8, 19:8-10, 16:11-15, 26:27-29)

So from these few examples we clearly see that those Jesus trained (the Apostles) and those trained by others practiced at least the first tactic of the Ministry Multiplication Cycle. They constantly sowed the gospel and reaped new believers. But what about the other tactics? Were these practiced as well? Let's turn our attention to the establishing tactic.

Establishing

Let's again start with the Apostles. Did they practice the two steps of the establishing tactic, baptizing and teaching?

Remember after Peter's first evangelistic message that three thousand people came to Christ. What happened to them? Acts 2:41–42 tells us, "So then, those who had received his word were *baptized*; and that day there were added about three thousand souls. They were continually devoting themselves to the apostles' *teaching* and to fellowship, to the breaking of bread and to prayer." We are not sure who baptized these new believers. It seems doubtful that Peter did the baptizing alone since it would have taken fifty hours to baptize that many people if he only spent sixty seconds per person. If the rest of the apostles joined him, then the task of baptizing that many would have been manageable. We can assume that the apostles participated, but they may also have had help from some of the other 120 people (Acts 1:15) who had assembled before Pentecost. Though Scripture doesn't specify whether the apostles did the baptizing, verse 42 does clearly state that the apostles spent time teaching these new followers of Christ.

Acts 5:42 stresses the same idea: "And every day, in the temple and from house to house, they [the apostles] kept right on teaching and preaching Jesus as the Christ." We can conclude, therefore, that the apostles, after Jesus trained them, practiced the tactic of establishing.

Let's look at the ministries of Peter, Philip and Paul. Did they seek to establish new believers by baptizing and teaching them?

Luke makes no specific reference to Peter personally baptizing or teaching anyone in the book of Acts. In this book, Peter directs his sermons toward unbelievers. However, in the books of First and Second Peter, we clearly see Peter teaching believers how to grow in their faith. First Peter 2:2 exhorts followers of Christ to "long for the pure milk of the word that by it you may grow in respect to salvation." In the very last verse of his second epistle, Peter urges his readers to "grow in the grace and knowledge of our Lord and Savior Jesus Christ."

What about Philip? Luke writes of Philip baptizing the Ethiopian (Acts 8:38), but never mentions anything about Philip teaching new believers. Like Peter, when Philip preaches, he seems to direct his message toward outsiders. Acts 8:39 tells us that Philip "kept preaching the gospel to all the cities until he came to Caesarea."

What detail Luke may lack in his description of Philip's ministry, he makes up for it in his record of Paul's ministry. In Philippi, Paul baptized Lydia and her family (Acts 16:15) as well as the Philippian jailer and his family (Acts 16:33). In response to Paul's ministry in Corinth, "Crispus, the leader of the synagogue, believed in the Lord with all his household, and many of the Corinthians when they heard were believing and being baptized." According to 1 Corinthians 1:14, Paul personally baptized Crispus and Gaius. One other verse clearly shows that Paul practiced baptism. Acts 19:5 notes that in Ephesus, after Paul shared Jesus with some followers of John the Baptist, "they were baptized in the name of the Lord Jesus."

Paul, however, did not stop with baptizing new believers. In Antioch (Syria), Barnabas and Paul "met with the church and taught considerable numbers" for an entire year (Acts 11:25–26). In Lystra, Iconium and Antioch (Pisidia), Paul and Barnabas were "strengthening the souls of the disciples, encouraging them to continue in the faith" (Acts 14:21–22). Paul with the aid of Silas traveled "through Syria and Cilicia, strengthening the churches" (Acts 15:40–41). With Timothy's help, "churches were being strengthened in the faith" (Acts 16:5). For a year and a half, Paul taught the Word of God in Corinth (Acts 18:11). On a return trip to the Galatian region and Phrygia, Paul was "strengthening all the disciples" (Acts 18:23). Even the conclusion to the book of Acts shows Paul teaching about the Lord Jesus Christ (Acts 28:30–31).

Furthermore, consider the purpose behind the books of Romans, 1 and 2 Corinthians, Galatians, Ephesians, Philippians, Colossians, and 1 and 2 Thessalonians. Paul writes these books to establish these followers in their walk with God. Consider this small sampling:

- He writes in Romans: "For I long to see you so that I may impart some spiritual gift to you, that you may be *established*" (Rom. 1:11); and "Now to Him who is able to *establish* you according to my gospel and the preaching of Jesus Christ, according to the revelation of the mystery which has been kept secret for long ages past," (Rom. 16:25).

- He prays in 1 Thessalonians 3:13, "So that He may *establish* your hearts without blame in holiness before our God and Father at the coming of our Lord Jesus with all His saints."

- In Colossians 1:23 he writes, "if indeed you continue in the faith firmly *established* and steadfast, and not moved away from the hope of the gospel that you have heard, which was proclaimed in all creation under heaven, and of which I, Paul, was made a minister."

- And don't forget Colossians 2:7, a verse we've already seen, where Paul declares, "having been firmly rooted and now being built up in Him and *established* in your faith, just as you were instructed, and overflowing with gratitude."

The Ministry Multiplication Cycle

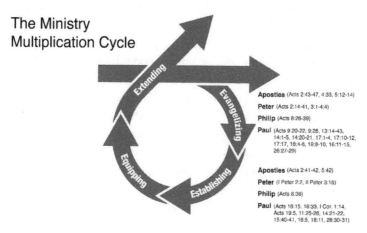

Apostles (Acts 2:43-47, 4:33, 5:12-14)

Peter (Acts 2:14-41, 3:1-4:4)

Philip (Acts 8:26-39)

Paul (Acts 9:20-22, 9:28, 13:14-43, 14:1-5, 14:20-21, 17:1-4, 17:10-12, 17:17, 18:4-8, 19:8-10, 16:11-15, 26:27-29)

Apostles (Acts 2:41-42, 5:42)

Peter (I Peter 2:2, II Peter 3:18)

Philip (Acts 8:38)

Paul (Acts 16:15, 16:33, I Cor. 1:14, Acts 19:5, 11:25-26, 14:21-22, 15:40-41, 16:5, 18:11, 28:30-31)

From this brief survey of Acts, we have no question that those Jesus trained (the apostles) and those trained by others, practiced establishing, the second tactic of the Ministry Multiplication Cycle.

Equipping

Do we see any clear evidence of the apostles raising up other workers? Not really. On the one hand, a case could be made that the seven deacons in Acts 6:1–6 show evidence that the apostles equipped other leaders. After all, two of the seven, Stephen and Philip, make huge impacts that Luke records in Acts chapters seven and eight. On the other hand, we don't know if Jesus or someone else initially equipped these men.

We do know, however, that people were learning how to proclaim the message of the gospel. Acts 8:1–4 tells us that the believers who left Jerusalem due to the persecution resulting from Stephen's message in Acts 7, traveled throughout the region of Judea and Samaria preaching the word. We would be safe to assume that the apostles had a role in equipping at least some of these pilgrims. It is an assumption, however, and not clear evidence.

The same is also true for Peter and Philip in the book of Acts. Nothing stands out. Things change dramatically, however, when we get to Paul. He is clearly selecting and mobilizing workers. Acts 14:21–23 describes Paul and Barnabas appointing and releasing elders in every church in Lystra, Iconium and Antioch (Pisidia). Again in Acts 20:17–35, Paul gives explicit instructions to the elders of the church in Ephesus. Not only does he review with them training he had previously provided for them, he also adds charges such as the one in verse 28, instructing them to "Be on guard for yourselves and for all the flock, among which the Holy Spirit has made you overseers, to shepherd the church of God which He purchased with His own blood."

If we leave the book of Acts for a moment, we find even more evidence of Paul intentionally training effective workers. In his letters to Titus and Timothy, he shares in great detail how they can be more effective in their ministries. In fact, in 2 Timothy 2:2 Paul famously declares, "The things which you have heard from me in the presence of many witnesses, entrust these to faithful men who will be able to teach others also." Paul challenges Timothy to multiply more and more workers.

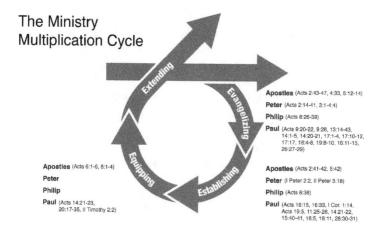

The Ministry Multiplication Cycle

Extending

Evangelizing

Equipping

Establishing

Apostles (Acts 2:43-47, 4:33, 5:12-14)
Peter (Acts 2:14-41, 3:1-4:4)
Philip (Acts 8:26-39)
Paul (Acts 9:20-22, 9:28, 13:14-43, 14:1-5, 14:20-21, 17:1-4, 17:10-12, 17:17, 18:4-8, 19:8-10, 16:11-15, 26:27-29)

Apostles (Acts 2:41-42, 5:42)
Peter (I Peter 2:2, II Peter 3:18)
Philip (Acts 8:38)
Paul (Acts 16:15, 16:33, I Cor. 1:14, Acts 19:5, 11:25-26, 14:21-22, 15:40-41, 16:5, 18:11, 28:30-31)

Apostles (Acts 6:1-6, 8:1-4)
Peter
Philip
Paul (Acts 14:21-23, 20:17-35, II Timothy 2:2)

We can safely conclude that the early leaders of the Church practiced the Ministry Multiplication Cycle's tactic of equipping. That leaves one final tactic. Was the extending tactic also implemented?

Extending

Where do we find evidence of others in the book of Acts practicing the tactic of extending by challenging and sending others to cross cultural boundaries?

Even though Jesus stressed repeatedly that His disciples should take the message of God's love and forgiveness to the nations, nothing really happened the first seven to eight years after Jesus ascended into heaven. One primary reason for the Jewish Christians not to reach out to the Gentiles was a consequence of their Jewish background of cultural separation. Jews (and by extension, Jewish Christians) were believed to be clean, but the Gentiles, or Greeks as they were sometimes called, were considered unclean. We will get to this barrier of cultural exclusivity more in a moment when we talk about Peter and Cornelius in Acts 10.

So in the first nine chapters of the book of Acts, there's not much missionary activity. But once we get to Acts 11:19–24, things change quickly:

THE MINISTRY MULTIPLICATION CYCLE

So then those who were scattered because of the persecution that occurred in connection with Stephen [Acts
7:59—8:1] made their way to Phoenicia and Cyprus and
Antioch, speaking the word to no one except to Jews alone.
But there were some of them, men of Cyprus and Cyrene,
who came to Antioch and began speaking to the Greeks
also, preaching the Lord Jesus. And the hand of the Lord
was with them, and a large number who believed turned
to the Lord. The news about them reached the ears of the
church at Jerusalem, and they [the apostles] sent Barnabas
off to Antioch. Then when he arrived and witnessed the
grace of God, he rejoiced and began to encourage them all
with resolute heart to remain true to the Lord; for he was
a good man, and full of the Holy Spirit and of faith. And
considerable numbers were brought to the Lord.

From this passage we see that the apostles (after a slow start)
practiced the extending tactic by sending Barnabas to reach the
Gentiles of Antioch.

You may be wondering why earlier we used Philip
reaching the Ethiopian official in Acts 8 as an example
of evangelism but now we are using Peter reaching Cornelius the Roman Centurion in Acts 10 as an example of
extending. After all, both the Ethiopian and the Roman
are Gentiles, right? Correct. Ethnically they are both the
same; they are both Gentiles. Religiously, however, they
are very, very different. Even though both are seeking the
Messiah, one is Jewish and the other is Gentile.
The Ethiopian was a "proselyte," meaning that when
Philip met him on the road to Gaza that he had already
converted to the Jewish faith (Acts 8:27). The Ethiopian's
conversion to Judaism meant that he kept the Law of
Moses, which included circumcision. Religiously, the
Ethiopian was Jewish, not Gentile.
Cornelius, on the other hand, is a "God-fearer," meaning
that he is interested in the God of the Jews, but he had not
yet decided to convert to the Jewish faith (Acts 10:22).
Peter is about to show Cornelius that he can become a
follower of Christ without first converting to Judaism.

> This shortcut, so to speak, will shatter the thinking of
> the Christian leadership in Jerusalem when Peter returns
> and reports on his ministry to Cornelius and company.
> Up until this point the Christian leadership thought
> Gentiles had to first become Jewish before they could be-
> come followers of Christ. Culture is powerful as we shall
> see in the next chapter.

As a result of Peter's obedience, Cornelius and his guests not only hear, but also respond to Peter's presentation of the gospel (Acts 10:34–48). Imagine how elated Peter must have felt . . . that is, until he returns to Jerusalem. There he is initially rebuked by the Church leadership for meeting with the Gentiles (Acts 11:1–3). It is not until after Peter's explanation of his vision and visit that they finally realize that the gospel was for the nations, for everyone, including the Gentiles (Acts 11:18). In the very next paragraph beginning with Acts 11:19, the followers of Christ finally begin taking the good news to the Gentiles (Greeks). Though it took them seven to eight years to get going, under the apostle Paul's leadership they begin to spread the gospel throughout the Roman Empire. But we are getting ahead of ourselves. Let's first consider Philip. Did he practice the extending tactic?

Philip is one of the first to cross cultural boundaries to tell people about Christ when he travels to the city of Samaria in Acts 8:5–13. (Samaria at that point was both a city as well as a district, similar to New York City located in New York state.) Remember that the Samaritans were partially Jewish and partially Gentile. For that reason, when the church leadership in Jerusalem hears that the Samaritans had received the Word of God, they send Peter and John to investigate (Acts 8:14). Convinced and probably a bit amazed that Samaritans have come to Christ through Philip's proclamation, Peter and John also share the gospel with Samaritans on their return trip to Jerusalem (Acts 8:25). That brings us to Paul.

It is evident that Paul practiced the tactic of extending since he is famously known for his three missionary journeys. On his first missionary trip, Paul intentionally begins to focus on sharing the gospel with Gentiles. He quotes Isaiah 49:6 to justify his decision:

". . . we are turning to the Gentiles. For so the Lord has commanded us, 'I have placed You as a light for the Gentiles, that You may bring salvation to the end of the earth'" (Acts 13:46b-47). As a result, the Lord uses him and Barnabas to plant churches in four cities in the eastern part of what we know today as the country of Turkey.

You would think that the leaders of the church would have greatly rejoiced when Paul and Barnabas later return to Jerusalem and report the huge response to the gospel by the Gentiles. After all, these leaders had previously blessed Peter's outreach to the Gentiles at Cornelius's house in Acts 10-11. Unfortunately, you would be wrong. Some of the leaders still have trouble with the concept that Gentiles did not have to first become culturally Jewish before they could become followers of Christ. Their mentality changes, however, after a big debate in Acts 15. James, the half-brother of Jesus and the foremost leader of the church in Jerusalem, finalizes the decision to permit Gentiles to become followers of Christ without first becoming Jewish. He quotes Amos 9:2 to show the biblical rationale: "So that the rest of mankind may seek the Lord, and all the Gentiles who are called by My name."

Soon Paul leaves on his second missionary trip, this time to the area of the world which we know today as Greece. Not long after that trip, Paul leaves for a third missionary trip. On this last trip, he travels to Ephesus, located in the western part of modern day Turkey. On each of these trips, Paul again plants churches among the Gentiles.

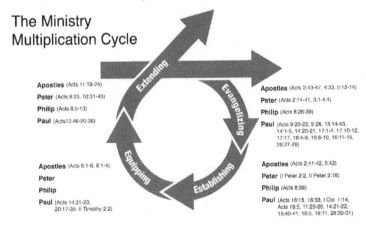

The Ministry
Multiplication Cycle

Extending

Apostles (Acts 11:19-24)
Peter (Acts 8:25, 10:31-45)
Philip (Acts 8:5-13)
Paul (Acts 13:46-20:38)

Evangelizing

Apostles (Acts 2:43-47, 4:33, 5:12-14)
Peter (Acts 2:14-41, 3:1-4:4)
Philip (Acts 8:26-39)
Paul (Acts 9:20-22, 9:28, 13:14-43,
14:1-5, 14:20-21, 17:1-4, 17:10-12,
17:17, 18:4-8, 19:8-10, 16:11-15,
26:27-29)

Equipping

Apostles (Acts 6:1-6, 8:1-4)
Peter
Philip
Paul (Acts 14:21-23,
20:17-35, II Timothy 2:2)

Establishing

Apostles (Acts 2:41-42, 5:42)
Peter (I Peter 2:2, II Peter 3:18)
Philip (Acts 8:38)
Paul (Acts 16:15, 16:33, I Cor. 1:14,
Acts 19:5, 11:25-26, 14:21-22,
15:40-41, 16:5, 18:11, 28:30-31)

Let's return to the question we asked at the beginning of this chapter. If the Ministry Multiplication Cycle is truly a biblical strategy, shouldn't we see it replicated by those Jesus trained? Having finished our brief survey of the book of Acts, we can definitively declare that the people Jesus trained followed the Ministry Multiplication Cycle.

	Apostles	Peter	Philip	Paul
Evangelizing	Acts 2:43–47, 4:33, 5:12–14	Acts 2:14–41, 3:1—4:4	Acts 8:26–39	Acts 9:20–22, 9:28, 13:14–43, 14:1–5, 14:20–21, 17:1–4, 18:4–8, 19:8–10, 16:11–15, 26:27–29
Establishing	Acts 2:41–42, 5:42	1 Pet 2:2, 2 Pet 3:18	Acts 8:38	Acts 16:15, 16:33, 19:5, 11:25–26, 14:21–22, 15:40–41, 16:5, 18:11, 28:30–31
Equipping	Acts 6:1–6?, 8:1–4?			Acts 14:21–23, 20:17–35, 2 Tim 2:2
Extending	Acts 11:19–24	Acts 8:25, 10:31–45	Acts 8:5–13	Acts 13:46–20:38

At the risk of sounding like a voiceover from a late-night commercial, it must be added, "Wait! There's more!" It gets even better. Not only did the implementation of the Ministry Multiplication Cycle result in the multiplication of Christians, it resulted in the multiplication of churches. This observation revolutionized my thinking. Let me explain.

Paradigm Change in My Thinking

Since I did not attend church growing up, I was not very familiar with the multitude of roles in which a "professional minister" could serve. (I like to differentiate between professional ministers and ministering professionals. I think Scripture teaches that we are all called to minister, some as professional ministers and some as ministering professionals.) I was aware of only three types of professional ministers: pastors, music ministers, and youth ministers. I knew I did not want to be the senior pastor of a church because my perception at the time was that pastors of churches were always going to hospitals or officiating funerals, neither of which seemed appealing to me as a teenager. Others assured me that I should not pursue becoming a music minister, although I personally thought my monotone sounded wonderful. Though I really wasn't that attracted to youth ministry, I was seeing a lot of students pray to receive Christ. As a result of the fruit, I thought that was where I should serve. And I did, for several years. During that time, the youth ministry grew from 40 students participating weekly, to over 200.

One morning during the Christmas holidays, I closed the cover of the book I had just finished reading and declared, "That's what I am supposed to do!" The book was about church planting: going to places where access to the gospel was lacking, leading people to Christ, helping them grow in spiritual maturity and raising up other workers and leaders to help. The very next day a dear friend called to ask if I would be willing to help him with a church plant in Atlanta. Thirteen weeks later, my wife and I, along with our four month old baby relocated. Everything I had learned about ministry converged. I was evangelizing, establishing and equipping others for the purpose of starting a culturally contextualized fellowship in an area of Atlanta with tens of thousands of unchurched people.

We led scores of people to Christ and I was having the time of my life. That is, until those three graduates from Columbia International University (the ones I mentioned earlier) showed up and challenged me about pancakes and waffles. Not only did I realize that I needed to focus on missions mobilization–or what we are calling extending–but also I realized that there were many, many places around the world with far less access to the gospel. And these places represented billions of people.

When I realized how many people needed to hear the good news of God's love and forgiveness in Christ, I was overwhelmed. Almost immediately I realized that God was calling me to help do something about the need. (That calling launched Crossover Global, which multiplies church planters to plant multiplying churches. But that's another story.) I also realized that multiplying Christians was not going to be enough to reach the world for Christ. We needed to multiply churches, thousands and thousands of churches. Without churches, believers would tend to be overcome by their surrounding culture.

You cannot believe the elation I felt during a time of Bible study when I discovered that when the Christ-followers in the book of Acts implemented the Ministry Multiplication Cycle, they not only multiplied Christians, they also multiplied churches . . . all over the known world. Here's what I found.

Multiplication of Churches

As we saw in our walk through the Gospels, Jesus took the Twelve through the Ministry Multiplication Cycle and then ascended into heaven. Let's call this first cycle the Dominical Cycle. (*Dominus* is Latin for master or lord. So the Dominical Cycle represents the Lord's cycle.)

After Jesus ascends into heaven, the apostles take the people of Jerusalem through the Ministry Multiplication Cycle, which results in the church of Jerusalem. In broad strokes, they evangelize (Acts 2:1–40), establish (Acts 2:41–5:42), equip (Acts 6:1–9:42) and extend (Acts 10:1–11:18). Let's call this cycle the Apostolic Cycle.

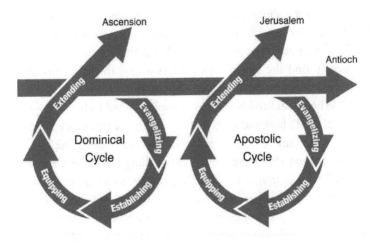

At Acts 11:19, we see the third cycle. Previously while the apostles remained in Jerusalem and continued their ministry to the church there, other believers fled to Antioch, Syria because of the persecution that arose in connection with Stephen. Once in Syria a new cycle, the Antiochian Cycle, begins resulting in the church of Antioch. Note the four tactics. We find these Christians evangelizing (Acts 11:19–24), establishing (Acts 11:25–26), equipping (Acts 13:1 shows the various leaders that have emerged), and, finally, extending (Acts 13:2–4) as they launch Barnabas and Paul on their first mission trip.

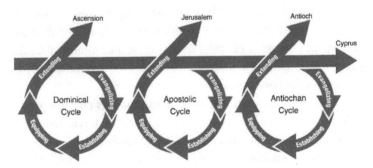

Once the church of Antioch mobilizes Barnabas and Paul, the momentum for church planting accelerates. During that first missionary trip, churches are planted in Derbe, Lystra, Iconium and Antioch (in the district of Pisidia). The second missionary trip results in church plants in Philippi, Thessalonica, Berea, Athens and Corinth. During his third missionary trip, Paul plants the church in Ephesus. Let's call this generation of church planting the Pauline Cycle.

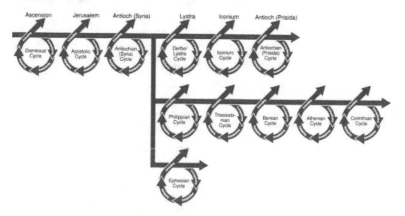

If you leave the book of Acts and go to the book of Colossians, you'll find another generation of churches multiplying from the church in Ephesus. Paul's teammate, Epaphras, leaves the church in Ephesus to plant churches in Colossae, Laodicea and Hierapolis (see Colossians 1:7, 2:1, 4:12–13). At the risk of making up a new word, let's call this generation of church planting the Epaphrian Cycle. The map on page 75 shows the geographical locations of these various church plants.

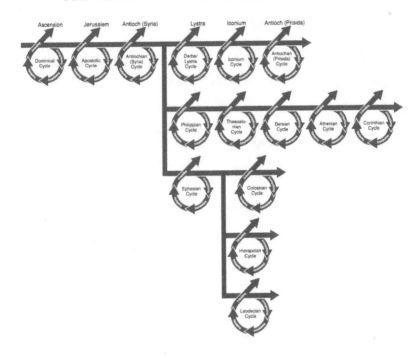

And the process has continued through the ages, sometimes more effectively than at other times. Christians multiplying Christians. Churches multiplying churches. And it all started with Jesus. Yet, it could all end with us. As it has been said many times, Christianity is just one generation away from extinction. But Jesus has left us a powerful strategy, the Ministry Multiplication Cycle.

Before we get too excited, we must ask another question. Will the Ministry Multiplication Cycle "work" in other cultures? Granted it worked two thousand years ago in a Greco-Roman culture. But will it work today? Can the Ministry Multiplication Cycle prove effective today at reaching privileged urban youth in the United States as well as, say, the Muslims of North Africa who may be living in utter destitution? We agree the Ministry Multiplication Cycle is biblical, but is it cross-cultural? Let's probe this question in the next chapter.

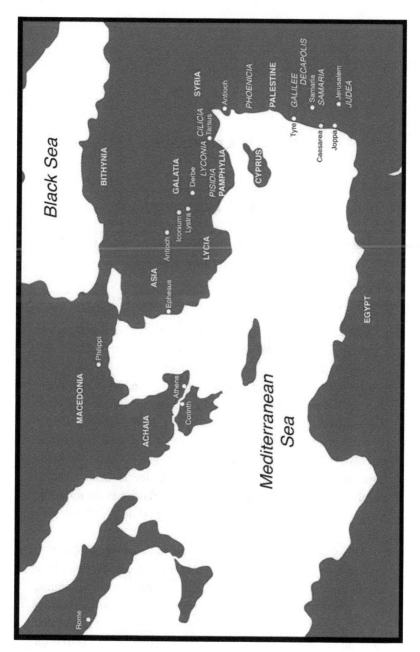

The Roman World during the New Testament

Chapter 5

Cultural Perspective

Will the Ministry Multiplication Cycle Work in Different Cultural Contexts?

CULTURE IS VERY POWERFUL. Sometimes our cultural perspective exerts such a strong influence that it controls our thoughts and actions even more than God's Word does. We saw an example of this tendency in the previous chapter. The Lord Jesus repeatedly told the twelve disciples to take the message of forgiveness to all nations, to every people group. Yet seven to eight years after Christ gave this great commission, when Peter finally arrived at the house of Cornelius, Peter stated that it was not lawful for him to be at his house since Cornelius was not a Jew. Peter's Jewish culture had so deeply permeated his thinking that he was blinded to the opportunity he had to reach this Gentile with the good news of the gospel. Culture is very powerful.

In 1987 Joao Mordomo and I founded Crossover Global with the desire to mobilize this generation for the evangelization of the world. As the Soviet Union and Eastern European communist block began disintegrating, we focused our efforts on planting churches to reach the millions of people who had been taught that God did not exist. I remember being invited to teach a course on religion at a university in St. Petersburg, Russia. About the second or third day, the students commented that I was teaching the course like I actually believed in God. It was a joy to see many of those students come to understand and believe the truth after being presented with the evidence for God's existence as manifested in the death, burial and resurrection of Jesus Christ.

By 1994 we had chosen Moldova, one of the fifteen republics of the former Soviet Union, as the first country where we would send missionaries to start churches. We chose Moldova because at the time the city of Moscow already had 600 missionaries, whereas the entire country of Moldova only had six missionaries.

As we traveled the country trying to determine where the greatest needs were found, we talked to pastors of churches that managed to survive the difficult years of persecution under the communist government. My life was greatly changed for the better as I talked to aged men and women who suffered great torment because of their stand for Christ. My heart was set aflame as I listened to the price they paid to spread the message of Christ. One conversation was indelibly etched on my mind. A young man named Peter told me how he traveled deep into Russia to reach people for Christ. He lived in a small town but would walk to nearby villages in order to spread the gospel. Some nights the tremendous snowfalls would keep him from reaching the warmth and safety of his home. In order to survive he would dig a hole in the snow, similar to an igloo, and crawl inside. Though it was warmer in the hole than outside, he was still surrounded by snow! As a result, he lost several toes to frostbite, a small price to pay from his perspective.

I share this story to emphasize how the churches there possessed something promoted by Scripture, but tends to be missing from churches in our own culture–commitment. Unfortunately, however, those churches had added other things that are not found in Scripture. Please understand that my next comments are not meant to belittle these believers. These pastors and I had many healthy conversations about the role and impact of culture. I am just trying to make the point that culture is very powerful. So what are some of the additions that my Moldovan friends attached to church life that they were convinced were absolutely true and necessary?

First, I learned that I had better not clap in a church service. Now, I kind of like to clap. I am actually pretty good at it. I clap much better than I sing. We were told, however, that if anyone clapped in church, that they would lose their salvation. They informed us that if any of the new Christians ever smoked, they would lose their salvation. (Full disclosure: When I was ten years old, I did try one puff of rabbit tobacco. If you grew up in the country you know what I'm talking about. That horrible experience immediately cured me from ever wanting to smoke in the future.) If any of the women wore makeup, they would lose their salvation. If the new churches didn't have windows, then they were not really churches. If you didn't clasp your hands in front of you during prayer, then you were not really praying. The list goes on.

It is easy to understand why they held some of these beliefs and practices as though they were scriptural. Since the communists were imprisoning pastors, destroying Bibles, closing seminaries, and denying educational opportunities to children of believers, the few remaining church leaders tended to be uneducated. The average pastor had only an eighth grade education. These church leaders believed that if they could just keep their flocks faithful, they could survive. And survive they did, but they added a lot to church life that originated from their cultural perspective, not from Scripture.

You can understand why there might be misunderstandings between the "old" believers worshipping in churches which had survived Communism and the "new" believers coming to faith in Christ in the new churches we were planting among secular young adults raised in an atheistic environment. Culture is very powerful.

We have found these cultural add-ons everywhere we've gone. For example, some of the strongest followers of Christ living in Azerbaijan believed that their gathering was not yet a "real" church because someone told them that they had to have a pulpit in order to be a real church. Where does one find that in Scripture? Imagine at Pentecost after the three thousand people had responded to the gospel, Peter stopping everything and saying, "Wait! We can't go any further until we have a pulpit. Quick! Who knows how to build a pulpit, a really big one?" Again, I am not trying to make fun of anyone. I am trying to make a point: Culture is very powerful!

This reality leads us to an important question. Will the Ministry Multiplication Cycle work in different cultural contexts? In other words, is the Ministry Multiplication Cycle relevant for today? Could it be that it was effective during the days of Jesus and the apostles because of the pervasive and unifying Greco-Roman culture, but we should no longer consider using it today because contemporary culture has become so diverse? Does age make a difference? Does a people group's ethnicity change the strategy? Surely one size does not fit all!

These are great questions and in a very real sense, all are true. The Ministry Multiplication Cycle will NOT work if you think only in terms of practices.

May we use our sanctified imaginations for a moment? Try to imagine what it was like when Billy Graham arrived in heaven and met Philip (the person in Acts 8 who ran up to the chariot of the Ethiopian official and led him to Christ). Do you think that after a brief introduction and some appropriate niceties, Billy told Philip that if he had quit chasing chariots and began preaching in stadiums, that Philip would have been much more effective in reaching people for Christ? As they politely argued, do you think one stressed his numeric success, while the other passionately noted which method was actually found in the Bible and which one wasn't? Pretty farfetched, right? You can be quite confident, however, that neither chariot-chasing nor stadium-preaching methodologies would be effective today in a culture hostile to the Christian faith.

Back to our question. Will the Ministry Multiplication Cycle work in different cultural contexts in light of how powerful culture can be? The answer is "no," if you think only in terms of practices as our absurd illustration on Billy Graham and Philip highlights. Yet if you think in terms of principles, the answer is a resounding "yes!" The Ministry Multiplication Cycle becomes very effective regardless of the host culture.

What's the difference between a principle and a practice? A principle is a biblical truth relevant for all cultures at all times. A practice, on the other hand, is a ministry method that may only be effective for a given group of people at a given time in history.

Biblical Principles	Ministry Practices
General	Specific
More hidden	More obvious
Foundational	Operational
Guided by biblical content	Guided by cultural context
Never changes	Constantly changing
Effective for all cultures	Tend to be effective for a specific culture
Timeless	Tend to be effective for a specific time

Let's look at a couple of examples to make sure we understand the difference. Take the biblical principle of Scripture distribution. We see this principle often in Scripture. One example is found in Colossians 4:16: "When this letter is read among you, have it also read in the church of the Laodiceans; and you, for your part read my letter that is coming from Laodicea." How has the practice of Scripture distribution changed over time? In Paul's day Scripture was disseminated on parchment. Later believers distributed Scripture by pen and paper. That practice drastically changed with the printing press. The practice has changed repeatedly with the invention of billboards, radio, records, television, cassette tapes, computers, floppy disks, CDs and apps for mobile phones. It won't be long before we could have animated holograms of biblical authors reading their book of the Bible to us. While the practice of

Scripture distribution has greatly changed over time, the principle of Scripture distribution has not changed at all.

Consider another example. This time let's inspect the biblical principle of Christians assembling for the purpose of worship. One sees this principle in many passages of the Bible, but few as clearly as Hebrews 10:25, which exhorts, "not forsaking our own assembling together, as is the habit of some . . ." Do church gatherings look the same in every culture? Most people reading this verse might imagine a church service with a large crowd sitting comfortably in pews or chairs within a building with regulated heat and air-conditioning, loudly singing hymns from hymnals or choruses projected onto a screen and listening to a sermon amplified by a microphone and speakers. Assemblies such as these may be common in the West, but are non-existent in cultures that persecute Christians. In those places you might find people who sneak into a small apartment by ones and twos, singing in whispers and trying to understand the incomplete portions of Scripture that they have in their possession. The principle of assembling together is occurring in both cultures, but the actual practices could not be any more different.

There's a well-known proverb that goes like this:

> Methods are many.
> Principles are few.
> Methods often change.
> Principles never do.

When it comes to practices and principles, we could change the wording to this:

> Practices are many.
> Principles are few.
> Practices always change.
> Principles never do.

With this understanding between the difference between a principle and a practice, let's consider how the Ministry Multiplication Cycle can be effective in every culture, regardless of time and place.

Biblically Sound Ministry Principles

As we begin to identify some key biblical principles, let's recall what we've covered up until this point. In chapter 1, we gained an understanding of the flow of Jesus' ministry. By the end of chapter 2, we saw that there was a strategy to Jesus' ministry and it contained four fundamental tactics: evangelizing, establishing, equipping and extending. As we moved through chapter 3, we used four key passages from the gospels to spotlight ten practical steps illustrated in the diagram below:

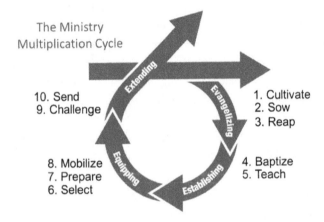

The Ministry Multiplication Cycle

10. Send
9. Challenge

Extending

Evangelizing

1. Cultivate
2. Sow
3. Reap

8. Mobilize
7. Prepare
6. Select

Equipping

Establishing

4. Baptize
5. Teach

Chapter 4 provided us with a parentheses. We paused to gain assurance that we had indeed found a biblical strategy. We did this by confirming that the people Jesus trained, and the people who they in turn trained, implemented the same strategy. Now in chapter 5, we are trying to discern principles that will help us effectively implement Jesus' strategy of multiplication in whatever culture we find ourselves ministering.

To keep from being overwhelmed, we will limit ourselves to just a few examples of principles taken from the exact same scriptural passages from which we identified our ten steps. Let's start with the passage in John 4:1–42. Here are some of the principles that seem to jump off the page for me.

Cultivating Principles
(from John 4)

- Jesus looked for ways to be with unbelievers: "And He had to pass through Samaria." (v. 4). Jesus did not *have to* pass through Samaria on His trip from Judea to Galilee because of a lack of other alternate routes. He could have easily used the popular Transjordan Highway to circumvent the despised Samaritans. He *had to* pass through Samaria because He had a divine appointment with the unbelieving Samaritans. We, too, should creatively look for opportunities to be with unbelievers.

- Jesus initiated relationships with unbelievers: "There came a woman of Samaria to draw water. Jesus said to her, 'Give me a drink'" (v. 7). As verse 27 indicates, at that time in history it was not culturally proper for a man to initiate a conversation with a woman. Yet Jesus knew she needed living water. We need to initiate relationships with non-Christians if we are to share the gospel with them.

Sowing principles
(from John 4)

- Jesus listened for spiritual needs: "'Our fathers worshiped in this mountain, and you people say that in Jerusalem is the place where men ought to worship.' Jesus said to her, 'Woman, believe Me, an hour is coming when neither in this mountain nor in Jerusalem will you worship the Father'" (vv. 20–21). We often tend to do all the talking when we find ourselves with outsiders. Jesus, on the other hand, did more listening than talking. As the conversation between the Samaritan woman and Jesus continued, the Lord listened for comments that showed the woman's spiritual temperature. In the same way, we need to keep our ears open to needs or questions that provide us an opening to communicate the gospel.

- Jesus communicated spiritual answers: "The woman said to Him, 'I know that Messiah is coming (He who is called Christ); when that One comes, He will declare all things to us.' Jesus said to her, 'I who speak to you am He'" (vv. 25–26). Jesus did not hesitate to share the good news about who He was, and He did so without making the woman feel condemned by Him. We should do the same.

Reaping principles
(from John 4)

- Jesus understood that many people are ready to give their lives to God: "Do you not say, 'There are yet four months, and then comes the harvest'? Behold, I say to you lift up your eyes and look on the fields, that they are white for harvest'" (v. 35). Jesus had an optimistic perspective. He knew that many people's hearts longed to personally experience God's love and forgiveness. We, too, should be confident that even today God has many people ready to be harvested for the Kingdom. We need to extend the invitation to them to cross over into a right relationship with Christ.

- Jesus capitalized on natural relational networks: "Many more believed because of His word; and they were saying to the woman, 'It is no longer because of what you said that we believe, for we have heard for ourselves and know that this One is indeed the Savior of the world'" (vv. 40–41). After the woman at the well received His offer of Living Water, Jesus spent time ministering in the woman's sphere of influence. As He did, many more gave their lives to Him. Likewise, we can see many more believe in Christ as we become friends with the friends of new believers.

Overall Strategy	Four Tactics	Ten Steps	Biblical Principles
Ministry Multiplication Cycle	Evangelizing (John 4:1–42)	Cultivate	Look for ways to be with unbelievers. Initiate relationships with unbelievers.
		Sow	Listen for spiritual needs. Communicate spiritual answers.
		Reap	Realize that many are ready to come to Christ. Take advantage of relational networks.
	Establishing (Matthew 28:19–20)	Baptize	
		Teach	
	Equipping (Mark 3:14)	Select	
		Prepare	
		Mobilize	
	Extending (Luke 24:46–48)	Challenge	
		Send	

Baptizing Principles
(from Matthew 28)

- Jesus valued baptism: "Baptizing them in the name of the Father and the Son and the Holy Spirit" (Matt 28:19). Jesus' value of the importance of baptism can be seen several places throughout the gospels: His own baptismal experience with John the Baptist, His ministry of baptizing others (John 3:22, 4:1–2), and His command for His followers to continue baptizing others after He was gone. We should place a similar value on baptizing people in our ministries.

Teaching Principles
(from Matthew 28)

- Jesus taught His followers: "All that I commanded you . . ." (v. 20). Jesus taught His followers what they should know about God and His Word as well as how they should live their lives in a way to honor God. We need to do the same.

- Jesus focused on the application of Scripture, not just the information: "Teaching them to observe . . ." (v. 20). Throughout His ministry, Jesus clearly emphasized obedience, not just outward obedience, but obedience from the heart. We, too, need to ensure that the people in our ministries personally apply the biblical content that we teach.

Overall Strategy	Four Tactics	Ten Steps	Biblical Principles
Ministry Multiplication Cycle	Evangelizing (John 4:1–42)	Cultivate	Look for ways to be with unbelievers. Initiate relationships with unbelievers.
		Sow	Listen for spiritual needs. Communicate spiritual answers.
		Reap	Realize that many are ready to come to Christ. Take advantage of relational networks.
	Establishing (Matthew 28:19–20)	Baptize	Value baptism.
		Teach	Teach the Scriptures. Focus on application, not just information.
	Equipping (Mark 3:14)	Select	
		Prepare	
		Mobilize	
	Extending (Luke 24:46–48)	Challenge	
		Send	

Selecting Principles
(from Mark 3)

- Jesus prayed all night before selecting His future leaders: "And He went up on the mountain and summoned those He Himself wanted" (v. 13). To fully understand this phrase, we need to look at the parallel passage in Luke 6:12–13, which says, "It was at this time that He went off to the mountain to pray, and He spent the whole night in prayer to God. And when day came, He called His disciples to Him and chose twelve of them . . ." Jesus realized that He needed to select very carefully those who would carry on the task of world evangelization after He was gone, so He prayed all night before making the decision. We, too, must carefully select the people we want to train to serve in our own ministries. If we choose unwisely, we will waste much time and effort. We need God's guidance in selecting potential workers.

- Jesus chose a limited number to be with Him: Mark writes "And He appointed twelve" (v. 14). Interestingly, Jesus chose only twelve people from a multitude of prospects, even though He had the world to reach. Obviously, the more workers and leaders, the better chances the church has to make a difference. The quality of the workers needed, however, reduced the quantity of the workers Jesus could train. When it comes to thoroughly training future workers, we need to select an appropriate number. Leaders cannot be mass produced. Attempting to train too many at one time can severely diminish our effectiveness.

- Jesus intimately knew those He chose to equip: "He . . . summoned those He Himself wanted, and they came to Him" (v. 13). Remember from our harmony of the gospels, that Jesus was halfway through His approximately three-year ministry at this point. Recall also that He met these followers at the beginning of His ministry and had been on extended ministry trips with many of them prior to selecting them to serve as part of the Twelve. We can get ourselves and our ministries in a lot of trouble if we select people for training we don't know and it turns out that they are not ready.

Preparing Principles
(from Mark 3)

- Jesus showed the Twelve what it means to do the work of the ministry: "that they would be with Him . . ." (v. 14). Because Jesus lived with the Twelve for approximately one and a half years, they not only listened to His words, they also watched His life. They saw Him heal the sick, preach and teach the Word, cast out demons, perform miracles, share the message of love and forgiveness both to Jews and Gentiles, pray to God and serve others. Truly more is caught than taught. We also need to pour our lives into the people we are equipping. We need to spend an ample amount of time with them so they can see us doing the ministry, not just talking about it.

Mobilizing Principles
(from Mark 3)

- Jesus involved the Twelve in His ministry: "and that He could send them out to preach . . ." (v. 14). After watching Jesus do the work of the ministry, the Twelve soon found themselves getting hands-on experience. Three chapters later, at the beginning of Mark 6, we find Jesus sending His men in ministry teams of two to preach, heal and cast out demons. A few verses later, we find these teams reporting to Jesus all they had accomplished. We provide our own teams with great equipping opportunities when we let them participate in the work of the ministry. Helping them to process their successes and failures will make them much more effective.

Overall Strategy	Four Tactics	Ten Steps	Biblical Principles
		Cultivate	Look for ways to be with unbelievers.
			Initiate relationships with unbelievers.
	Evangelizing (John 4:1–42)	Sow	Listen for spiritual needs.
			Communicate spiritual answers.
		Reap	Realize that many are ready to come to Christ.
			Take advantage of relational networks.
Ministry Multiplication Cycle	Establishing (Matthew 28:19–20)	Baptize	Value baptism.
		Teach	Teach the Scriptures.
			Focus on application, not just information.
	Equipping (Mark 3:14)	Select	Pray before selecting potential workers.
			Limit how many potential workers you choose.
			Make sure you know the potential workers well.
		Prepare	Demonstrate to emerging workers how to minister to others.
		Mobilize	Involve prepared workers in actual ministry.

Overall Strategy	Four Tactics	Ten Steps	Biblical Principles
Ministry Multiplication Cycle	Extending (Luke 24:46–48)	Challenge	
		Send	

Challenging Principles
(from Luke 24)

- Jesus constantly cast a world vision: "and that repentance for forgiveness of sins should be proclaimed in His name to all the nations . . ." (v. 47). Throughout His ministry, Jesus stressed the need for all the people groups of the world to know the gospel. Consider His ministry with the Samaritans in John 4 or His outreach to the Syrophoenician (Gentile) woman in Matthew 15. Yet the more equipped the Twelve became, the more Jesus emphasized their responsibility to take the message of the gospel to the ends of the earth. In our own ministries, we need to continually focus on the need for all nations to know the love and forgiveness of Christ.

- Jesus also kept the Twelve focused on the spiritual needs right in front of them: "beginning from Jerusalem." (v. 47). Although Jesus wanted His ministry team to "tell of His glory among the nations, His wonderful deeds among all the peoples," He did not let them lose sight of the spiritual needs surrounding them. Sometimes we get so caught up in reaching the world for Christ that we forget about the unbelievers living next door or across the street from us. We need to challenge the people in our ministries to have a heart for people, all people.

Sending Principles
(from Luke 24)

- Jesus entrusted the Twelve with the responsibility of spreading the gospel, announcing that "You are witnesses . . ." (v. 48). Jesus made sure that His team knew it was their responsibility to share the gospel. He repeatedly told them that they were now responsible for going and for telling. The Twelve were to be the witnesses. We must impart the same kind of commitment to the people God has called us to serve. Reaching the world requires a team effort. A one-man-show won't do it.

- Jesus empowered the Twelve with the Holy Spirit: "I am sending forth the promise of My Father upon you; but you are to stay in the city until you are clothed with power from on high" (v. 49). Jesus knew His followers could not take the gospel to the ends of the earth in their own strength, regardless of how gifted they might be. God's work could only be accomplished in the power of the Holy Spirit. The Lord clearly communicated that to fulfill the heart of God, they needed to be filled with the Spirit of God. We, too, must make sure that the World Christians we send to the nations know how to appropriate, by prayer and faith, the power of the Holy Spirit.

Overall Strategy	Four Tactics	Ten Steps	Biblical Principles
		Cultivate	Look for ways to be with unbelievers. Initiate relationships with unbelievers.
	Evangelizing (John 4:1–42)	Sow	Listen for spiritual needs. Communicate spiritual answers.
		Reap	Realize that many are ready to come to Christ. Take advantage of relational networks.
Ministry Multiplication Cycle	Establishing (Matthew 28:19–20)	Baptize	Value baptism.
		Teach	Teach the Scriptures. Focus on application, not just information.
	Equipping (Mark 3:14)	Select	Pray before selecting potential workers. Limit how many potential workers you choose. Make sure you know the potential workers well.
		Prepare	Demonstrate to emerging workers how to minister to others.
		Mobilize	Involve prepared workers in actual ministry.

Overall Strategy	Four Tactics	Ten Steps	Biblical Principles
			Give your team a vision for reaching the world.
		Challenge	Keep the team focused on meeting the spiritual needs surrounding them.
Ministry Multiplication Cycle	Extending (Luke 24:46–48)		Impart to your team members a heart-felt responsibility for taking the gospel to the world.
		Send	Launch World Christians who know how to accomplish God's goals by appropriating the Holy Spirit's power.

The above discussion articulates just a few biblical principles from just four passages of Scripture. The principles in and of themselves are nothing spectacular. Yet in a very simple way, they are very powerful.

What do we mean by that? Have you ever taken a ministry problem to a seasoned effective Christian worker? Maybe it had been a while since you had seen any outsiders crossing over into a relationship with Christ and you wondered what was wrong. You questioned your friend, searching for answers. Your mentor responded with something like, "Are you looking for ways to be around seekers?" Or, "Are you building any friendships with outsiders?" Wide-eyed you responded, "You're right! Why didn't I see that! You are so wise!" Simple, but powerful.

Typically, mentors and consultants communicate in principles. They are smart enough, or at least experienced enough, not to give a one-size-fits-all answer. What makes the mentor so wise is that he or she has learned to look at situations through the lenses of principles.

Culturally Relevant Ministry Practices

With an understanding of the importance of biblical principles, we are ready to discuss the scariest topic of this book, practices. Unfortunately, it is here that most people want to start. They beg to be told what to do. Or, they copy a successful ministry that they admire, thinking that they will have the same results. Inevitably, they are disappointed. Sometimes it is because they are not as gifted or do not have the same resources as the minister or ministry they are trying to emulate. Other times, however, the failure is due to one thing: Culture is powerful! They try to implement a practice that is not relevant to their cultural context.

In the next chapter, we will explore the implementation of biblical principles like those above. We will find that the resulting ministry practices, even though they may be based on similar biblical principles, can widely differ in execution depending on the cultural context. Culture is that powerful, but the Ministry Multiplication Cycle of Jesus is that adaptable!

Chapter 6

Personal Perspective

What Might the Ministry Multiplication Cycle Look like in Your Cultural Context?

I TRULY HESITATED TO include this chapter for several reasons. First, as mentioned last chapter, some ministry leaders, due to a lack of time, training or motivation just want to emulate another's ministry. That approach might work, but chances are that the leaders are positioning the ministry for failure. Not sharing any practical illustrations, however, leaves the book too theoretical and abstract. So please read this chapter cautiously.

As mentioned in the introduction (I told you that you should have read the introduction.), Crossover Global began in our basement thirty years ago. Focused solely on church planting, Crossover Global currently ministers in about 40 countries representing numerous cultural contexts. The vast majority of the 2000 plus new churches that we have started were planted among predominantly Muslim and Hindu people groups. During this time, I have lived in the USA. Though I minister cross-culturally several times each year, I am involved week to week in reaching the people in my own community in my own cultural context. Initially I involved myself with college students. Later I devoted myself to reaching the business community.

Let's look at how the Ministry Multiplication Cycle accomplishes the same results in these drastically different contexts by using biblically sound principles expressed in culturally appropriate practices. Let's look at different ministries for college students, then for businessmen, and lastly for the mission field. We will organize the ministries around the four tactics of Jesus' multiplication strategy.

College Students

After the pastor of our large downtown church in Columbia, South Carolina asked my sweet wife and me to serve the college students of our church, we couldn't wait to meet them. At the first Sunday School class there were five "students" and seven adults. I place the word students in quotation marks because two of them were 30-year-old males attending the class in order to pickup young females. The following Sunday, after I made friendly phone calls to the two 30-year-olds, we had three students and seven adults. We had our work cut out for us.

Evangelizing Ministries

Sunday Night Alive

It took over a year, but the college students who had come to know the Lord and had grown in their walks with God caught a vision of taking their campuses for Christ. The students formed a student organization at the large public university located just a few blocks from our church and started a program called Sunday Night Alive. The format of the "show" was based on the long-running television show, Saturday Night Live. Each week a strong Christian with high visibility on campus hosted the show. The first fifty minutes included hilarious skits and popular music. During the final ten minutes, the host shared how he or she had crossed over into a personal relationship with Christ.

When the show was over, we served free pizza. Paying for the food quickly exhausted the college budget, but when the church saw college students coming to Christ, they gladly increased the amount allocated. While students were eating pizza, the student leaders would sit with visitors and ask four questions:

1. Did you enjoy the show?
2. What did you think of the host's spiritual journey?
3. Has anything like that ever happened to you?
4. Would you like to learn how you also can cross over into a personal relationship with Christ?

Depending on the answer, the student leaders would share the gospel. All around the auditorium you could see the gospel being diagramed on napkins and pizza box tops. It was quite exciting!

The first night we had 103 in attendance. (Full disclosure: The very first show was a huge flop. The students asked me to speak on finances. They thought every college student would be interested in that topic. They were, but not enough to come to the show. They preferred listening to one of their peers.) As we learned culturally relevant ways to reach secular students, the crowds grew quickly. As time passed, Sunday Night Alive reached over 500 college students every Sunday night. The ministry lasted twelve years and dozens of students accepted Christ each year. Some of these students later found themselves serving in churches or on the mission field.

Student Surveys

Another evangelistic ministry that brought great fruit was walking around campus and asking students if they would take two minutes to answer a survey about their spiritual condition. Some weren't interested. Some, however, were eager to express their opinions. Many came to Christ through these surveys. Many others heard about Sunday Night Alive and started attending regularly.

Establishing Ministries

Bible Studies

As students started coming to Christ, we immediately set up Bible studies on campus. Though we never fulfilled it, our vision was to have a weekly Bible study in every dorm, fraternity and sorority on campus.

Sunday School

If the emphasis of Sunday Night Alive was on "go and tell," the emphasis of Sunday School was on "come and see." The student leaders viewed the Sunday School hour as a way to help secular students who had given their lives to Christ begin attending church on Sundays. To make the ministry more culturally attractive, we completely overhauled our church's practice of hosting a college Sunday School class. We moved from a dingy classroom to a large updated venue. Student leaders welcomed new guests at the door and then walked them to a huge assortment of food and drinks that the ladies of the church prepared for us each week. From there they accompanied visitors to one of the many tables and sat with them for the rest of the hour so the guest would never feel alone or out of place. The program included student-led worship, student stories of how Christ was working in their lives, and strong Bible teaching.

Equipping Ministries

Leadership Training Group

On Wednesday nights, we trained the student leadership. This group consisted of the 30–40 student leaders who helped lead Sunday Night Alive, Sunday School, student surveys and the Bible studies. The meeting lasted for two hours. We spent the first thirty minutes eating pizza (we ate a lot of pizza) and evaluating the previous Sunday Night Alive's show. The next thirty minutes we spent on our knees or faces as we prayed for God to impact the college students of our city. The final sixty minutes we used to train student leaders how to share the gospel (see Appendix C), teach a Bible study, or disciple a young believer.

Extending Ministries

Short-term Mission Trips

During the summers we travelled with students on short-term mission trips. We used these trips to give them a heart for the nations. At minimum, those who went returned with a greater appreciation for how God had blessed them.

A Ministry Overview to College Students.

Three years after serving in the college ministry of my local church, my mother developed cancer. My family needed me, so I took a leave of absence from the college students. A year later, I was again ready to serve. To my surprise, rather than sending me back to work with the students I loved so much, God sent me in a different direction.

Businessmen

Not long after traveling back and forth from Columbia, South Carolina, to Atlanta, Georgia to help care first for my mother and then, after mom's battle with cancer, to care for my dad, I received a call from a dear friend. He had recently experimented with an outreach to businessmen in our city and he wanted me to assist him with the next one by helping answer Bible questions. He called the event a Roundtable discussion. Although I didn't know what to expect, I accepted the invitation. When the event was over, my heart was captured. I knew God wanted me to shift my focus at home from college students to businessmen.

Evangelizing Ministries

Roundtable Discussions

Although we constantly tweak this outreach to the business community, the basic structure has remained unchanged for some time. Five of us form the leadership core of the group. My friend, whom I am convinced knows everyone in the city, serves as the host. Another friend and I serve as the "answer people." Due to his high profile in our city, the fourth friend serves as the bait. Many of our guests attend these roundtables just to meet him. The fifth team leader is one who has recently come to Christ and exhibits that passionate exuberance that tends to characterize new believers.

We invite nine to eleven men we think are seeking a genuine relationship with God to join us in a conference room, not a church building. Remember that we are trying to reach outsiders. We learned this important factor early on when one invitee said he would never step foot in a church. We tell the invitees that the group is a private meeting where men gather to ask questions that they would like answered about God or religion. To our surprise, hundreds of men have accepted the invitation.

Since the meeting begins shortly after work, we provide dinner in the form of sandwiches from a deli. (Note: This ministry works well in Columbia, South Carolina, because of the size of our city. Most people who work in downtown Columbia can get anywhere in the area within 30 minutes. This ministry might not work in Atlanta since it is hard to get anywhere in less than an hour. Keep in mind that effective ministries must be contextualized for the culture because culture is powerful!) We meet from 6–8 p.m., starting on time and ending on time. We know that since Columbia is so small, if we ever let the meeting run overtime word would spread and in the future men would be reluctant to attend.

We organize the meeting around three questions. While the men eat their sandwiches, I begin by asking the question, "Using football as an analogy, where are you in your spiritual journey?" Over the years we have heard some quite creative responses.

Next we ask, "What are your questions this evening?" We unashamedly use the Bible to answer their questions. We even make available multiple copies of the same version of the Bible so we can tell the men to turn to page xx, rather than tell them to turn to Second Timothy 1:9–10. This has proven very helpful since most of the men do not know their way around in the Bible. As we answer questions, we talk a lot about biblical and cultural "Christians." If at the end of the meeting no one has asked about the difference between a biblical and a cultural "Christian," one of the core group members may ask us to elaborate. This practice allows us to share the gospel as we explain that a person may look like a Christian on the outside, but not possess Christ on the inside.

By 7:35 p.m., we shift to the third question for the night by asking, "What insights are you taking away from the meeting?" Depending on how they answer this last question, determines what step we take next.

Evangelistic Appointments

If we think a guest at the Roundtable seems open to further conversation about the things of God, we initiate getting together for breakfast or lunch. During the meal we ask these questions:

1. What did you think of the Roundtable discussion?

2. Have you thought much about the difference between being a biblical Christian and a cultural Christian?

3. Have you crossed over into a personal relationship with God or are you still in the process?

4. Would you like to hear what Scripture has to say about beginning this personal relationship?

If the person seems eager to know more about a relationship with Christ, we share the gospel with them. (See Appendix C for the method we use to share the gospel.)

Establishing Ministries

Bible Studies

Two weeks after the first Roundtable discussion, I met one of the attendees for lunch. Clearly God was working in his life. At the end of our meal, I shared the gospel with him and asked him if he saw anything keeping him from crossing over into a right relationship with God. He said he wasn't ready. I was convinced that he was very close. Back at his office he called his godly wife. She asked him if he had accepted Christ while at lunch with me. When he said he had not, his wife told him not to come home until he had. (I am not necessarily recommending this approach to evangelism, although it did happen to work!) He walked a couple of blocks to his church, found an unlocked door, slipped into the sanctuary, got on his knees and invited Christ into his heart. He actually prayed twice just to make sure he was doing it correctly! When he arrived home, his wife took one look at his face and said, "You are different!" He was. Christ had changed him.

The next day when I heard the news, I knew he was only the first of many new believers to come. I believed my teammate had stumbled onto a culturally relevant way to share the gospel with the businessmen in our city using the roundtable format. That conviction led us to launch a Bible study. Since that first Bible study we have started dozens of Bible studies over the years for new believers as well as for others who want to grow spiritually.

To make these Bible studies accessible to the business community, we offer them during breakfast and lunch. Remember that in our city of Columbia, people can get anywhere fairly quickly and easily. The major part of our city is only ten city blocks by ten city blocks. As groups have multiplied, Bible studies can be found almost anywhere, at any time. Our vision is to offer Bible studies every day on every city block.

The format is simple. Most of the groups tend to be small, closed groups. A closed group means that membership in the group is by invitation only. We have also experimented with large, open groups. Large, open groups offer much more energy and excitement, but the impact on lives tends to be less. We often say, "We can make a good impression from up front. Yet, to make a lasting impact, we need to get up close."

Some of the groups have been together for almost twenty years. Other groups meet for an agreed upon number of weeks or months. A dear friend and I study with ten to twelve men for two years. They join the group with the expectation that when the study ends that they will either start another Bible study, or help someone else start another Bible study. Over the two years, we read through the entire Bible chronologically using as a guide the series *Putting Together the Puzzle of the Old Testament* and *Putting Together the Puzzle of the New Testament*. We have developed 87 lessons that take approximately two years to complete due to summers and holidays. At present, the group I am currently leading will multiply into possibly seven new groups in just a few months.

Growth Groups

We have just spent a year experimenting with a new establishing ministry, one we call a Growth Group. We start in August and end in June, meeting only once per month. The first meeting involves introductions and an overview of the time together. The next eight months we focus on growing together in specific areas of our walks with God. The areas may vary from group to group depending on the needs of the individuals. Our recent group selected these topics: purpose in life, Scripture, prayer, marriage, walking in the Spirit, temptation, evangelism and stewardship. Between meetings we read one book and memorize one to two verses of Scripture related to the topic. We also accomplish a practical project between the meetings. For example, for the topic of prayer we develop a prayer journal. The month we study marriage, we take our wives on a date, look her in the eyes and tell her ten reasons why we love her.

Equipping Ministries

Leadership Training

Much of the leadership training for this men's ministry is organic. Many of the leaders come from groups we have led. After seeing the ministry in action, they leave to reproduce it. To guide the movement, the various leaders of the Bible studies meet together every spring and fall to provide updates and keep everyone tracking with the vision.

Teacher Training

Over the years we found some of the Bible study leaders struggling. They had the vision and commitment to help take our city for Christ, but lacked the necessary skills to teach others effectively. We address this need by offering teacher training. An attorney who is very gifted both at teaching as well as training others how to teach, offers intensives on the basics of teaching the Bible.

Extending Ministries

Bottom line: Many of the men have begun to give sacrificially to ministries that focus on reaching the nations. Apart from that, we have failed miserably at mobilizing businessmen for world evangelization. Pretty embarrassing. So, let's move on.

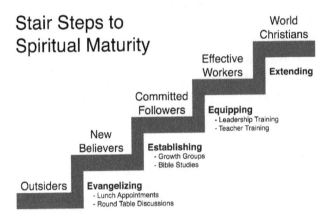

Stair Steps to Spiritual Maturity

Outsiders — **Evangelizing**
- Lunch Appointments
- Round Table Discussions

New Believers — **Establishing**
- Growth Groups
- Bible Studies

Committed Followers — **Equipping**
- Leadership Training
- Teacher Training

Effective Workers — **Extending**

World Christians

Ministry Overview to Businessmen

As you compare the ministries for college students with the ministries for the businessmen, you will notice the same biblical tactics of Jesus' multiplication strategy, but different expressions, depending on the cultural relevance. Most businessmen would not want to stay up late to watch their friends put on funny skits. Nor would they want to eat pizza at every meal. When you compare the Bible studies for the college students with Bible studies for the businessmen, you'll find that even though the same material may be covered, the wheres and whens are completely different. The students might meet in a dorm room at 11:30 at night with no set ending time. The businessmen, however, would rather meet at a restaurant or in a conference room with a clearly defined starting and stopping time.

Granted, this is pretty obvious stuff. After all, we are comparing college students with businessmen. Yet even though most ministry leaders see the cultural differences between students and adults generally speaking, they fail to consider the various nuances that occur between college ministry on small rural campuses versus large urban campuses, or between ministry to the business community in mega-cities versus small towns, whether the city is located in the north or in the south. One size does not fit all.

Culture is powerful. We must diligently search for ministries that not only are biblically sound, but also culturally relevant.

Let's see how the four tactics of the multiplication strategy play out in other countries.

Cross-cultural Church Planting

Crossover Global focuses on planting churches among unreached people groups with little or no access to the gospel. To better understand who these peoples are, think THUMB: Tribal–Hindu–Unreligious–Muslim–Buddhist. Most of the churches we have started are located in Hindu and Muslim cultural contexts. If you think that it is a challenge to implement effectively the Ministry Multiplication Cycle in these contexts in culturally relevant ways, you are correct. We are constantly learning and continually changing methods, yet never straying from biblical principles.

Although the following evangelizing ministries seem very generic, the establishing, equipping and extending ministries are, for the most part, quite unique.

Evangelizing Ministries

Medical Outreach

We sent our first missionaries to Moldova, a former republic of the once mighty Soviet Union, a few years after the communist empire collapsed. One of the most effective evangelistic ministries we initially offered was to provide medical teams and outdated but still effective medicines donated by pharmaceutical companies. Many people had physical problems due to the inadequate care available in this "new" country. After the teams provided medical care, our missionaries would share the gospel. This ministry worked well until the government declared that all doctors had to be certified by the Moldovan government and all medicines had to be current. When they changed, we changed.

Secret Outreach

After a few years in Eastern Europe primarily reaching people who for years had been indoctrinated by communist propaganda declaring that God did not exist, we began sending missionaries to Central Asia to live and serve among Muslims. Because of persecution we could not be as public with sharing the gospel as we had done in the Eastern European country of Moldova. We have had many teammates threatened, some jailed, several beaten, one stabbed and another stoned.

Since trust is of paramount importance, all of our outreach occurs one-on-one. Those who come to Christ often must worship in secret, arriving at a private house by ones and twos over a stretch of time, then singing in whispers so as not to draw attention.

Street Preaching

When our missionaries entered India, they found that street preaching proved effective. One of the biggest problems in a Hindu context is not getting to the people or proclaiming the gospel, but making sure that those who respond are not just adding Jesus to the other 33,000,000 Hindu gods that they worship. So, in India, we must devote much more attention to making sure that people understand the preeminence of Christ. Spiritual warfare is also very prevalent, so we make prayer an even greater emphasis there.

Establishing Ministries

Christian Leadership Training Program

Once our missionaries gather enough people to start a church, they begin culturally relevant establishing ministries such as Bible studies and discipleship groups. This stage of church planting can overwhelm a church planter resulting in numerical growth as well as spiritual depth plateauing. We realized quickly that we could accelerate the numerical and spiritual growth of these churches by providing an establishing ministry where churches from a whole region could send qualified members.

We call this opportunity the Christian Leadership Training Program. Depending on the cultural context, we offer the Christian Leadership Training Program either in a one-week format, which lasts all day from Monday to Friday, or over a period of four weekends.

Below you will find the content that they receive over a one to two-year period of time.

Christian Leadership Training Program

	CLTP - Year One	CLTP - Year Two
Module 1	Glorifying God in Life and Ministry	Defending the Faith (Apologetics)
Module 2	Building the Church	Walking in the Spirit
Module 3	Knowing the Faith (Doctrine)	Leading Biblically
Module 4	Enriching Marriages and Families	Learning the Ministry Multiplication Cycle

Few of the missionaries or the indigenous leaders involved in our movement can provide this level and quality of training on a consistent basis without help. Having the Christian Leadership Training Program as a resource has strengthened our new churches considerably.

Equipping Ministries

Church Planters Training Program

When the church members approach the end of the Christian Leadership Training Program, we intentionally expose them to a vision for church planting. Those who seem strongly motivated in multiplying new churches and who possess the necessary character and gifting are recruited to participate in our Church Planters Training Program.

Structured very similarly to the Christian Leadership Training Program, the Church Planters Training Program imparts the skills necessary to plant new churches.

Church Planters Training Program

	CPTP - Year One	CPTP - Year Two
Module 1	Planting Churches	Mobilizing People for Missions
Module 2	Understanding & Sharing the Gospel	Studying & Understanding the Old Testament
Module 3	Making Disciples	Studying & Understanding the New Testament
Module 4	Developing Leaders	Teaching & Preaching the Bible

Mentoring

Information is one thing: application is another. Once a person begins to plant a church, we assign them a mentor who meets with them a minimum of once per month. The mentor helps the new church planters to implement what they learn during the CPTP as well as manage the weekly problems that occur in ministry. Mentoring seems to be our secret sauce.

Extending Ministries

Cross-Cultural Workers Training Program

Few churches commission large numbers of people for missionary service. It appears that explosive missions mobilization does not happen by accident. This observation caused us to start a third training track. We called it the Cross-Cultural Workers Training Program. (By the way, we are pretty good at training others, but we are not very creative at naming things.) The chart below gives an overview of some of the areas we seek to impart to these future cross-cultural workers.

Cross-Cultural Workers Training Program

	CWTP - Year One	CWTP - Year Two
Module 1	Cross-Culturally Living	Cross-Cultural Communication
Module 2	World Religions	Muslim/Hindu Evangelism
Module 3	History of Missions	Contextualization
Module 4	Unreached People Groups	Ministry Multiplication Cycle

Mobilizing people we have reached to reach other cultures has greatly advanced the gospel. For example, we have seen Eastern Europeans plant churches in Central Asia. We have also witnessed some of the Central Asians reached plant churches in China. Church planting should be from the reached to the unreached, not just from the West to the rest.

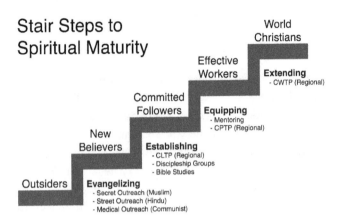

A Ministry Overview to Unreached People Groups.

Totally Different, Yet Very Much the Same

As you can see from the above, the three different groups needed completely different ministries. The Sunday Night Alive ministry would never work in Central Asia to reach Muslims in areas where persecution runs high. There evangelism must be accomplished in secret. Though these ministries look differently, they remain very much the same in that they both seek to reach people with the gospel of Christ's love and forgiveness. Each is totally different, yet very much the same. This brings us back to the main point of this chapter: the Ministry Multiplication Cycle can accomplish the same kinds of results in drastically different contexts by using biblically sound principles expressed in culturally appropriate ministries.

What culturally appropriate ministries, or practices, would you consider for your own personal ministry? You could place them in the Stair Steps diagram as we did previously or place them below in the chart we have been building throughout the preceding chapters. The Stair Steps diagram tends to help in communication to others. The chart, on the other hand, helps one not lose sight of the big picture.

Overall Strategy	Four Tactics	Ten Steps	Biblical Principles	Ministry Practices
Ministry Multiplica-tion Cycle	Evangelizing (John 4:1–42)	Cultivate	Look for ways to be with unbelievers.	???
			Initiate relationships with unbelievers.	???
		Sow	Listen for spiritual needs.	???
			Communicate spiritual answers.	???
		Reap	Realize that many are ready to come to Christ.	???
			Take advantage of rela-tional networks.	???
	Establishing (Matthew 28:19–20)	Baptize	Value baptism.	???
		Teach	Teach the Scriptures.	???
			Focus on application, not just information.	???
	Equipping (Mark 3:14)	Select	Pray before selecting potential workers.	???
			Limit how many poten-tial workers you choose.	???
			Make sure you know the potential workers well.	???
		Prepare	Demonstrate to emerg-ing workers how to minister to others.	???
		Mobilize	Involve prepared work-ers in actual ministry.	???

Overall Strategy	Four Tactics	Ten Steps	Biblical Principles	Ministry Practices
		Challenge	Give your team a vision for reaching the world.	???
			Keep the team focused on meeting the spiritual needs surrounding them.	???
Ministry Multiplication Cycle	Extending (Luke 24:46–48)	Send	Impart to your team members a heart-felt responsibility for taking the gospel to the world.	???
			Launch World Christians who know how to accomplish God's goals by appropriating the Holy Spirit's power.	???

We now have one more question: "Where should someone start if he or she wants to implement the Ministry Multiplication Cycle?" Let's address that question in the next chapter.

Chapter 7

Missional Perspective

Where Do We Begin in Order to Implement the Ministry Strategy of Jesus?

REMEMBER MY STORY FROM chapter 3 when I took three high school students on a retreat to help them catch a vision for reaching their campus for Christ? My intentions were fantastic, but the intended results were marginal at best. My point is that great intentions do not guarantee effective ministries. We must seek to implement ministries that are both biblically informed and culturally relevant.

By biblically informed, we mean that not only is our doctrinal statement based on Scripture, but our ministry strategy is as well. We must base our ministry tactics, steps, principles and practices on the ministry strategy of Jesus.

By culturally relevant, we mean that we strive to make our ministry practices meaningful to the people God has called us to serve. We cannot assume that replicating an effective ministry practice from another situation will prove effective in our own location because our cultural context may be very different. It is incumbent upon us tirelessly to search for those expressions of truth that powerfully impact those we are trying to reach.

So where do we start in order to implement the ministry strategy of Jesus? It depends. Determining where to begin depends on whether you are starting a new ministry or on whether you are strengthening an existing ministry. Since most people already serve in existing ministries, let's begin there.

Strengthening Existing Ministries

To implement the Ministry Multiplication Cycle in an existing ministry, many have followed this three-part approach. First, evaluate the ministry. Next, determine your direction. Lastly, make the necessary changes. Let's walk through each of these phases.

Evaluate the Ministry

To better evaluate the current health of your ministry, keep three vital concepts constantly at the forefront of your mind. Avoid confusing:

- Activity with productivity
- Form with function
- Process with product

Let's consider the difference between activity and productivity. To be productive implies that you are making progress in accomplishing a goal. The ultimate goal of all ministry is to glorify God by fulfilling the Great Commission. Unfortunately, many church workers and leaders seem extremely busy, but not very productive. The ministries that they lead are making little to no progress at helping outsiders become new believers, new believers become committed disciples, committed disciples become effective workers, or effective workers become World Christians. They are active, but not productive.

As we evaluate our ministries, we must honestly consider whether or not we are making progress. We cannot allow the busyness of activity to mask the lack of productivity in our ministries.

This perspective is not meant to make us feel like failures; instead it helps us avoid sliding into complacency and encourages us to stay open to making needed changes.

We must also consider the difference between form and function. Let's use the tactic of evangelism as an example. Helping people cross over into a personal relationship with Christ is the *function* of evangelism. The expression of that process is the *form*. We alluded to this distinction in chapter 5 when we discussed biblical principles and cultural practices. If we do not keep this distinction clearly in mind, we will overlook ministries (forms) that need changing because they are no longer culturally relevant and, as a result, no longer effective. We mistakenly think that because a ministry (form) is well-loved and highly honored, it is off-limits to major changes. Remembering that the function and not the form of the ministry is of primary importance will allow us to make the necessary changes to become more effective.

Finally, we must realize the difference between process and product. In chapter 2 we used the words tactics and targets. Remember that the multiplication strategy of Jesus has five target groups: outsiders, new believers, committed disciples, effective workers and World Christians. These are the intended "products" we want to see in our ministries. The process of evangelism moves the outsider up the stair steps of spiritual maturity to a new believer. The process of establishing moves a new believer up the stair steps to a committed disciple. The process of equipping moves a committed disciple up the stair steps to an effective worker. The process of extending moves an effective worker up the stair steps to a World Christian. Each of these tactics or processes may consist of a variety of ministries, some of which are effective and some of which are not effective. By effective, we are not referring to how many people are attending a meeting. We are questioning whether the ministry is actually moving people up to the next stair step. Granted, certain ministries will always prove more effective than others. So we are not suggesting that certain ministries are "better" than others. What we are suggesting is the importance of wise stewardship. If we conclude that the ministry is culturally irrelevant and no longer moving people up the stair steps of spiritual maturity, then we should stop that ministry. We can then use resources, such as the people and the money previously devoted to that ministry, for something that may be more effective.

With these three vital concepts firmly in mind, we can begin the actual evaluation.

Step #1: Honestly determine the spiritual profile of each person in your ministry. In this way you will know where everyone falls on the Ministry Multiplication Cycle. If you have so many in your ministry that you don't know everyone, then ask other leaders such as Sunday School teachers and small group leaders to help. When you have a question about someone's profile, always assume they are closer to the beginning rather than at the end of the Cycle.

Step #2: List all the programs (practices) in your ministry and then identify the purpose of each program. By purpose, we mean which of the four tactics does the ministry seek to accomplish. You may find this frustrating because you may have a program you believe serves two or more functions. For example, you may have a meeting where you teach the Bible to help establish believers in their faith, but sometimes you see people pray to receive Christ. That may be confusing. I understand. You must, however, determine the *primary* function of the given program. You must narrow its focus to one purpose and one purpose only. Many leaders make the mistake of trying to accomplish several tasks with each program. Rarely are any of them accomplished with excellence.

Step #3: Using the information above, fill in the chart below.

Step #4: Analyze the above information by answering questions like the following:

- Which boxes are empty?
- Which programs are effective?
- Where are programs needed most?
- Where are programs offered that are not needed and if eliminated could result in extra resources for other programs?
- Which tactics need the most attention?

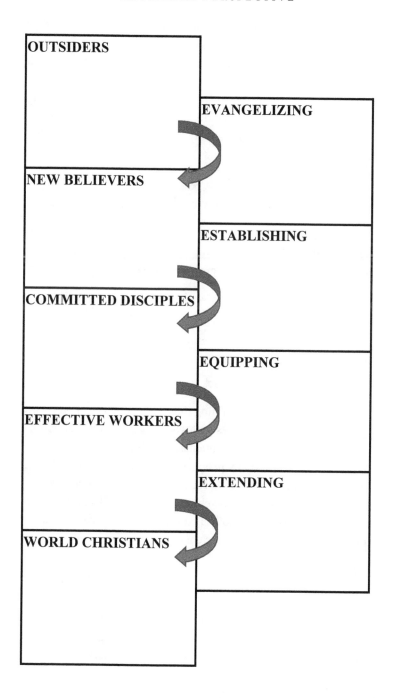

Spend a great deal of time in prayer asking God for wisdom both before and during this evaluation. Ask Him to open your eyes to the changes that you need to make in order to move people around the Ministry Multiplication Cycle. Do not let accepted, but ineffective, ministry practices bar you from searching for culturally relevant and biblically sound ministries that move people up the stair steps of spiritual maturity. Long to serve Christ as effectively as you can.

Determine your Direction

Using the above insights, next map out the top three changes you can make immediately that would make the biggest differences in your ministry. Keep the pointers below firmly in mind:

- Equipping people to be workers and leaders should be a priority.
- Eliminate as much duplication as possible, unless it is obviously effective.
- Strive for a balanced attack.

Take your time determining these three changes. If you have a leadership team that serves with you, make certain that you involve them in the process as much as possible.

Remember that many people do not respond well to change, so communication and timing are critical. Think through not only the changes you should make, but how you will communicate these changes, who needs to be involved in the changes, and when you should begin making these changes.

Make the Needed Changes

After determining your direction, begin implementing these strategic changes by assigning who makes which change, in what way, and by what day. Filling in a chart similar to the chart below might prove helpful.

	What?	How?	Who?	When?
Change #1				
Change #2				
Change #3				

Several months after making these changes, you may find it extremely helpful to repeat the three-part process of evaluating the ministry, determining your direction, and making the necessary changes. Since ministries often revolve around school calendars due to vacations and holidays, it might be helpful to go through this process during these three time periods: January to May, June to July and September to December.

Starting New Ministries

If we use the above steps for existing ministries, what do we do if we are starting with no ministry at all? The following suggestions should help.

Initial Approach

If you have just stepped off the plane into a completely new situation, do the exact same thing that Jesus did and later that the Twelve did. Assuming you have prepared just like Jesus and the Twelve, that is, you are prayed up and walking in the fullness of the Holy Spirit, you immediately begin with step one of the Ministry Multiplication Cycle. Later move to the succeeding steps as appropriate.

Step #1: Cultivate relationships with outsiders.
Step #2: Share the gospel in culturally relevant ways.
Step #3: Reap the fruit that is ripe.
Step #4: Baptize the new believers.

Step #5: Teach them how to become committed disciples.
Step #6: Select potential workers and leaders.
Step #7: Prepare emerging workers and leaders.
Step #8: Mobilize trained workers and leaders.
Step #9: Challenge effective workers to be World Christians.
Step #10: Send World Christians to serve as goers and senders.

Over time you will discern which ministry practices seem to be more effective than others. Give special attention to these programs.

Intermediate Approach

The moment the Lord provides potential workers and leaders, your focus needs to change. You still lead by example in terms of evangelizing and establishing, but now you must invest the majority of your time and energy into those who can multiply your efforts. You must now devote the greatest part of your time to equipping effective workers. The more workers and leaders you can develop, the greater impact you will make. Remember that you might be able to go faster alone, but you go further and last longer with a well-equipped team of effective workers.

Ultimate Approach

There comes a point when you are no longer starting a new ministry, but instead strengthening an existing ministry. When this time arrives, regularly go through the three-part process described previously for strengthening an existing ministry: evaluate the ministry, determine your direction and make the needed changes.

Continually bringing your ministry before the Father in prayer and seeking wisdom for your ministry from His Word will help you stay on mission as you do your part to reach the world for Christ. It is less likely that you will implement unbiblical approaches to your ministry, and you will also avoid sliding into cultural irrelevance.

Conclusion

OUR JOURNEY HAS COVERED a lot of ground in a short amount of time. Along the way, we have passed several significant mile markers. In chapter 1 we took a close look at the ministry of Jesus. We took the time to harmonize the four gospels into one unified narrative. We came away with a much better understanding of Jesus' ministry to the crowds and more specifically to the Twelve. We also gained greater insight into the chronological flow and geographical context of His ministry. Some of what we learned perhaps shattered what we may have been taught in Sunday School.

In chapter 2 we passed another mile marker when we answered the question, "So what?" We then looked at the information we discovered from Scripture (and not from somebody's book) in chapter 1 and found that Jesus had a clear strategy for His ministry. We gave it a name, the Ministry Multiplication Cycle. It consisted of four emphases, or tactics: evangelizing, establishing, equipping, and extending. These four tactics help people grow in terms of spiritual maturity. Evangelizing outsiders helps them become new believers. Establishing new believers helps them become committed disciples. Equipping committed disciples helps them become effective workers. Extending effective workers helps them become World Christians. Putting these four tactics and target groups together in a diagram produced what we called the Stair Steps to Spiritual Maturity.

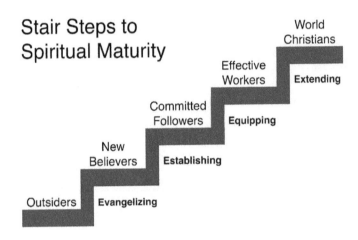

Stair Steps to Spiritual Maturity

Outsiders — Evangelizing
New Believers — Establishing
Committed Followers — Equipping
Effective Workers — Extending
World Christians

The Stair Steps diagram proved very helpful in visualizing Jesus' process of helping people grow in spiritual maturity, but it fell short of highlighting the power of multiplication inherent in that ministry. To help visualize that aspect of His ministry, we developed another diagram.

The Ministry Multiplication Cycle

We passed the third mile marker in chapter 3 when we identified at least ten practical steps in the ministry of Jesus. We said that the evangelizing tactic consisted of the steps of cultivating, sowing and reaping. We broke the establishing tactic into two steps: baptizing and teaching. The equipping tactic subdivided into selecting, preparing and mobilizing, while the extending tactic contained the steps of challenging and sending. We then added these steps to the Ministry Multiplication Cycle.

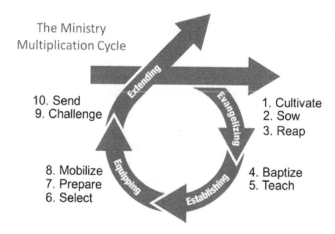

The Ministry
Multiplication Cycle

Extending
Evangelizing
Equipping
Establishing

10. Send
9. Challenge

1. Cultivate
2. Sow
3. Reap

8. Mobilize
7. Prepare
6. Select

4. Baptize
5. Teach

To determine whether the Ministry Multiplication Cycle was truly a biblical strategy, we searched the book of Acts to see if the people Jesus trained (or people trained by someone Jesus trained) actually implemented the strategy of Jesus. As we traced the ministries of Peter, Philip and Paul, the main characters in the book of Acts, we found clear evidence that all three practiced the four tactics of the strategy. As a bonus, this mile marker showed us that not only did the strategy multiply strong Christians, the strategy also multiplied strong churches.

The fifth mile marker showed us that the Ministry Multiplication Cycle is transcultural. That is, it can be effectively implemented in any cultural context as long as we think in terms of biblical principles and not ministry practices or methodologies.

Passing the sixth mile marker gave us a glance at how the strategy of Jesus has been practically implemented in a variety of cultural contexts. We looked at two North American situations, one among students and another among businessmen. We also looked at three church planting ministries, one among atheists in Eastern Europe, one among Hindus, and the other among Muslims living in Middle Eastern and Central Asian cultures. Finally, we left opportunity for you to develop your own biblically sound, culturally relevant ministry practices to implement in your own situation.

Overall Strategy	Four Tactics	Ten Steps	Biblical Principles	Ministry Practices
Ministry Multiplication Cycle	Evangelizing (John 4:1–42)	Cultivate	Look for ways to be with unbelievers.	???
			Initiate relationships with unbelievers.	???
		Sow	Listen for spiritual needs.	???
			Communicate spiritual answers.	???
		Reap	Realize that many are ready to come to Christ.	???
			Take advantage of relational networks.	???
	Establishing (Matthew 28:19–20)	Baptize	Value baptism.	???
		Teach	Teach the Scriptures.	???
			Focus on application, not just information.	???

Overall Strategy	Four Tactics	Ten Steps	Biblical Principles	Ministry Practices
Ministry Multiplication Cycle	Equipping (Mark 3:14)	Select	Pray before selecting potential workers.	???
			Limit how many potential workers you choose.	???
			Make sure you know the potential workers well.	???
		Prepare	Demonstrate to emerging workers how to minister to others.	???
		Mobilize	Involve prepared workers in actual ministry.	???
	Extending (Luke 24:46–48)	Challenge	Give your team a vision for reaching the world.	???
			Keep the team focused on meeting the spiritual needs surrounding them.	???
		Send	Impart to your team members a heart-felt responsibility for taking the gospel to the world.	???
			Launch World Christians who know how to accomplish God's goals by appropriating the Holy Spirit's power.	???

The seventh and final mile marker showed us how to begin implementing the Ministry Multiplication Cycle. We saw that if we are ministering in an established ministry, we should ideally begin by focusing on the equipping tactic. However, if we desire to launch a new ministry, we need to begin with the evangelizing tactic.

Common Questions

Though we have a much better understanding of the ministry strategy of Jesus and His desire to impact the world by multiplying His followers, we may still have many questions. As we close, let's look at some of the most commonly asked questions.

First, where does worship of God and fellowship with other believers fit in the Ministry Multiplication Cycle diagram?

Great question. Keep in mind that the Ministry Multiplication Cycle focuses on followers of Christ growing in spiritual maturity to a point where they can contribute to the ministry and have a heart for the nations. The intent of the Cycle is not necessarily meant to incorporate all the basic functions of a ministry.

With that said, you can show how worship and fellowship relates to spiritual growth by placing them in the middle of the cycle. Many prefer to show them in the form of a cross.

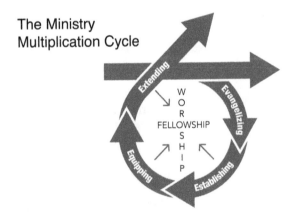

The Ministry
Multiplication Cycle

The thinking goes like this: Evangelizing only includes outsiders. Establishing only includes new believers. Equipping only includes committed disciples. Extending only includes effective workers. Worship and fellowship, however, include all followers of Christ. The newest believer can worship beside the most spiritually mature leader. Aged saints can fellowship with young children. All ground is level at the foot of the cross.

Second, where does prayer fit in the Ministry Multiplication Cycle diagram?

Simply put, everywhere! Every aspect of your ministry should be bathed in prayer, from planning to execution, from evangelizing to extending. Without prayer we have no power and we say to God that we can do the work of the ministry without Him.

Third, where does multiplication really occur, during the equipping tactic or during the extending tactic?

Another great question. Over the years, both in the classroom and in the field, this question has been asked repeatedly. It's been asked so many times that I realized that I needed to pay careful attention to this aspect of Jesus' strategy when training others. As a reminder, during the equipping tactic, Jesus was seeking to multiply and mobilize workers (and leaders, a particular category of workers) for ministry. During the extending tactic, Jesus was seeking to send workers to other cultures. A huge difference exists in what Jesus wanted to accomplish during the equipping tactic and the extending tactic.

Remember what you read in the introduction? The 200-plus countries of the world look more like waffles than pancakes. When we pour out the syrup of God's love and forgiveness on a country, the gospel does *not* spread to every part of the country. This failure is due to the communication barriers created by the cultural differences existing among the various ethno-linguistic people groups co-existing in that country. The syrup must be scooped up and carried across the cultural barrier and the good news communicated in a relevant way to the next group of people.

This concept implies that an entire people group in a country can be reached with the gospel-yet several other people groups in that same country can remain completely unreached. That is, unless ministries multiply (the equipping tactic) workers. Many of these new workers will remain and serve in their home cultures. Others, however, if challenged with a vision for the world, will want to go (the extending tactic) to the people groups around the world who have yet to hear the message of Christ in an understandable way.

Simply put, the emphasis of the equipping tactic is on multiplication and the emphasis of the extending tactic is on missions. Let's conclude with a few words on both the power of multiplication and the priority of missions.

The Power of Multiplication

The population of the world is growing exponentially. So if we are going to reach the world with the glorious good news of Jesus Christ, simply adding believers to the Kingdom is not fast enough. We must multiply. We must multiply by equipping more and more workers and leaders who in turn will evangelize, establish and equip others.

Multiplication is extremely powerful. This comment is not meant to distract from the power of the Holy Spirit or the power of prayer. By it, we mean to highlight this concept in the ministry strategy of Jesus. The following examples will demonstrate the explosive power of multiplication.

Did you know that you can become a millionaire in one month by simply putting one penny in the bank today and then doubling the amount you save every day for the next 30 days? Don't believe it? Take a look at the math.

Here's another example of the power of multiplication. Did you know

Day	Amount
1	$.01
2	$.02
3	$.04
4	$.08
5	$.16
6	$.32
7	$.64
8	$1.28
9	$2.56
10	$5.12
11	$10.24
12	$20.48
13	$40.96
14	$81.92
15	$163.84
16	$327.68
17	$655.36
18	$1,310.72
19	$2,621.44
20	$5,242.88
21	$10,483.76
22	$20,967.52
23	$41,935.04
24	$83,870.08
25	$167,740.16
26	$335,480.32
27	$670,960.64
28	$1,341,921.28
29	$2,683,842.56
30	$5,367,683.12
31	$10,735,366.24

that if you tore a page out of your Bible, which is approximately 1/500s of an inch thick, and folded it 64 times that it would be over 291 billion miles high? Don't believe it? Take a look at the math.

Folds	Inches	Feet	Miles
1	0.002	0.000	0.000
2	0.004	0.000	0.000
3	0.008	0.001	0.000
4	0.016	0.001	0.000
5	0.032	0.003	0.000
6	0.064	0.005	0.000
7	0.128	0.011	0.000
8	0.256	0.021	0.000
9	0.512	0.043	0.000
10	1.024	0.085	0.000
11	2.048	0.171	0.000

Folds	Inches	Feet	Miles
12	4.096	0.341	0.000
13	8.192	0.683	0.000
14	16.384	1.365	0.000
15	32.768	2.731	0.001
16	65.536	5.461	0.001
17	131.072	10.923	0.002
18	262.144	21.845	0.004
19	524.288	43.691	0.008
20	1,048.576	87.381	0.017
21	2,097.152	174.763	0.033
22	4,194.304	349.525	0.066

Folds	Inches	Feet	Miles
23	8,388.608	699.051	0.132
24	16,777.216	1,398.101	0.265
25	33,554.432	2,796.203	0.530
26	67,108.864	5,592.405	1.059
27	134,217.728	11,184.811	2.118
28	268,435.456	22,369.621	4.237
29	536,870.912	44,739.243	8.473
30	1,073,741.824	89,478.485	16.947
31	2,147,483.648	178,956.971	33.893
32	4,294,967.296	357,913.941	67.787
33	8,589,934.592	715,827.883	135.573

Folds	Inches	Feet	Miles
34	17,179,869.184	1,431,655.765	271.147
35	34,359,738.368	2,863,311.531	542.294
36	68,719,476.736	5,726,623.061	1,084.588
37	137,438,953.472	11,453,246.123	2,169.175
38	274,877,906.944	22,906,492.245	4,338.351
39	549,755,813.888	45,812,984.491	8,676.702
40	1,099,511,627.776	91,625,968.981	17,353.403
41	2,199,023,255.552	183,251,937.963	34,706.806
42	4,398,046,511.104	366,503,875.925	69,413.613
43	8,796,093,022.208	733,007,751.851	138,827.226
44	17,592,186,044.416	1,466,015,503.701	277,654.451

Folds	Inches	Feet	Miles
45	35,184,372,088.832	2,932,031,007.403	555,308.903
46	70,368,744,177.664	5,864,062,014.805	1,110,617.806
47	140,737,488,355.328	11,728,124,029.611	2,221,235.612
48	281,474,976,710.656	23,456,248,059.221	4,442,471.223
49	562,949,953,421.312	46,912,496,118.443	8,884,942.447
50	1,125,899,906,842.620	93,824,992,236.885	17,769,884.893
51	2,251,799,813,685.250	187,649,984,473.771	35,539,769.787
52	4,503,599,627,370.500	375,299,968,947.541	71,079,539.573
53	9,007,199,254,740.990	750,599,937,895.083	142,159,079.147
54	18,014,398,509,482.000	1,501,199,875,790.170	284,318,158.294
55	36,028,797,018,964.000	3,002,399,751,580.330	568,636,316.587

Folds	Inches	Feet	Miles
56	72,057,594,037,927,900	6,004,799,503,160.660	1,137,272,633.174
57	144,115,188,075,856.000	12,009,599,006,321.300	2,274,545,266.349
58	288,230,376,151,712.000	24,019,198,012,642.600	4,549,090,532.697
59	576,460,752,303,423.000	48,038,396,025,285.300	9,098,181,065.395
60	1,152,921,504,606,850.000	96,076,792,050,570.600	18,196,362,130.790
61	2,305,843,009,213,690.000	192,153,584,101,141.000	36,392,724,261.580
62	4,611,686,018,427,390.000	384,307,168,202,282.000	72,785,448,523.160
63	9,223,372,036,854,780.000	768,614,336,404,565.000	145,570,897,046.319
64	18,446,744,073,709,600.000	1,537,228,672,809,130.000	291,141,794,092.638

To put these distances in some kind of perspective, it helps to know that your stack of paper would be an inch high after your 10th fold and a foot high after your 14th fold. It would be over a mile high after your 26th fold. After the 44th fold you pass the moon, and after the 53rd fold you pass the sun. If you want to reach Pluto, you would need to fold your piece of paper 58 times. Amazing, isn't it?

In the above illustrations, we are only doubling. What if we tripled or quadrupled the numbers instead? The results truly become astronomical. Here's an even better question. What if we were tripling or quadrupling effective workers every year?

Let's start with tripling. Suppose you started today with three potential workers and every year you were able to triple that number by carefully equipping them for effective ministry. After one year you would have three teammates and in three years you would have twenty-seven. Imagine the impact you could make with twenty-seven effective workers in your ministry. If you quadrupled the number each year, then you would have four helpers after the first year and sixty-four helpers in three years. Again, multiplication is amazingly powerful.

Unfortunately, we often devote our energies to other activities. Three years later, we find ourselves in the exact same place that we started. We have done much, but perhaps accomplished little. But just imagine three or four years from now, if you just simply begin doubling leaders or locations! Would you dare to dream?

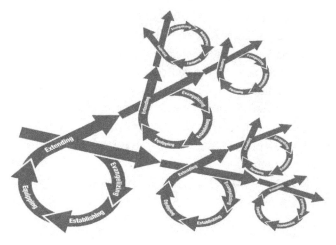

If we are going to reach the world, we must stay focused on multiplying large numbers of effective workers and leaders through the equipping tactic. Multiplication is amazingly powerful! Just amazing!

The Priority of Missions

That brings us to the priority of missions. Why should we even consider sending people across the ocean when spiritual needs exist across the street? Many reasons exist, all of which can be divided into two categories: those seen from a human perspective and those seen from a heavenly perspective. Let's consider a couple reasons from each perspective.

From a human perspective, the first reason we need to prioritize our mission efforts can be summarized in one word: access. In American culture, we have access to the good news. Think about the number of churches in your city, or the number of Christian radio stations or local parachurch ministries. We have the opportunity to hear the message of God's love and forgiveness repeatedly. Yet thousands of unreached people groups exist that have yet to hear even once the gospel of Jesus Christ because they have no churches. They have no translation of the Bible in their language. They have no Christian radio stations. They have no missionaries. They have no access to the gospel.

A second reason follows from the fact that many people groups have no access to the message of Christ. If someone dies without a personal relationship with God, Scripture says that they will spend eternity in hell suffering the consequences of their unforgiven sin. Second Thessalonians 1:8–9 puts it this way: upon His return, Christ will deal out "retribution to those who do not know God and to those who do not obey the gospel of our Lord Jesus. And these will pay the penalty of eternal destruction, away from the presence of the Lord and from the glory of His power." We need to make every effort possible for the sake of those who have yet to cross over into a right relationship with God through Jesus Christ.

From a heavenly perspective, we should diligently challenge the people in our ministries to go to the ends of the earth because God desires it. He has always desired to reconcile all people groups to Himself. We see this heart for the nations in Scripture from beginning to end. Many people mistakenly think that during the Old Testament God was concerned only for the Hebrews. They believe that God's heart for the Gentiles did not begin until the New Testament. Not so. Think about Adam and Eve. They weren't Hebrews. The Hebrew people group did not come into existence until Abraham. When the Hebrews did come into existence, God did not abandon His heart for the nations. Genesis 12:3 tells us that God was blessing the Hebrews in order to bless all the families of the earth, the Gentiles. That blessing was the coming Messiah. Halfway through the Old Testament Psalms 67:1-2 proclaims, "God be gracious to us and bless us and cause His face to shine upon us, that Your way may be known on the earth, Your salvation among all nations."

When we read the New Testament, we find Jesus repeatedly mandating His followers to go to the ends of the earth, to all the nations, in order to serve as His witnesses. At the very end of the New Testament, in Revelation 7:9 for example, we find "a great multitude which no one could count, from every nation and all tribes and peoples and tongues, standing before the throne and before the Lamb." In this passage, God's heart is ultimately fulfilled.

Furthermore, not only does God desire that we reach the nations, God also deserves that we reach the nations. God deserves our efforts to reach the unreached because of who He is and what He has done. He is *God*. And what did He do? He sent His Son to earth to die a sacrificial death for us in order to make a way for us to be reconciled to Him. What a glorious God we have!

With these last two thoughts in mind, the power of multiplication and the priority of missions, may we diligently implement the Ministry Multiplication Cycle, which Jesus modeled for us. May we evangelize outsiders so they become new believers, establish new believers so they become committed disciples, equip committed disciples so they become effective workers, and extend effective workers so they become World Christians. May we glo-rify our God and Father as we proclaim the Lord Jesus Christ in the power of the Holy Spirit.

Appendix A

Harmony of the Gospels
Summarized in 135 Key Events

Introduction

(Matt 1:1–25; Luke 1:1–80, 3:23–38; John 1:1–18)

I. The Private Period of Christ

Seven Groups
(From between 6–4 BC to AD 26)
(Matt 2:1—4:11; Mark 1:1–13; Luke 2:1–4:13)

A. Born to Mary and Joseph (Around 6–4 BC in Bethlehem) (Luke 2:1-7) 5

B. Worshiped by the shepherds (Around 6–4 BC in Bethlehem) (Luke 2:8-20) 6

C. Honored by Simeon and Anna (About six weeks later in Jerusalem) (Luke 2:21-40) 7

D. Sought by the Magi and Herod (At most two years later, probably in Bethlehem) (Matt 2:1-23) 8

E. Taught by temple teachers (Around AD 6–8 in Jerusalem) (Luke 2:41-52) 9

F. Baptized by John the Baptist (Late AD 26 in the Jordan River) (Matt 3:1-17; Mark 1:4-11; Luke 3:1-22) 10

G. Tempted by Satan (Late AD 26 in the wilderness) (Matt 4:1-11; Mark 1:12-13; Luke 4:1-13) 11

II. The Public Period of Christ

Seven Locations
(Matt 4:12–20:34; 26:6–13; Mark 1:14–10:52;
Luke 4:14–19:28; John 1:19–12:11)

A. A. Early Judean Ministry (Approx. Fall AD 26 to December AD 27) (John 1:19-3:36)

   1. In the city of Bethany beyond the Jordan (John 1:19-51) four days

      a. Confessed by John the Baptist as the Son of

III. The Trials Period of Christ

Seven Days (Passion Week)
(Matt 21:1—26:5, 26:14—27:66; Mark 11:1–16:1;
Luke 19:29–23:56; John 12:12–19:42)

IV. The Triumphant Period of Christ

Three Confidence Builders
(Matt 28:1–20; Mark 16:2–20; Luke 24:1–53;
John 20:1—21:25)

Appendix B

Harmony of the Gospels (Simplified)

Harmony of the Gospels (Simplified)

	Matthew	Mark	Luke	John
Introduction				
1. Purpose of the Gospels			1:1–4	
2. Prologue about Jesus				1:1–18
3. Predecessors of Jesus	1:1–17		3:23b-38	
4. Prophecies about John and Jesus	1:18–25	1:1–3	1:5–80	
Private Period				
1. Mary and Joseph			2:1–7	

Harmony of the Gospels (Simplified)

	Matthew	Mark	Luke	John
2. Shepherds			2:8–21	
3. Simeon and Anna			2:22–39	
4. Magi and Herod	2:1–23			
5. Temple Teachers			2:40–52	
6. John the Baptist	3:1–17	1:4–11	3:1–18, 21–23a	
7. Devil	4:1–11	1:12–13	4:1–13	
Public Period				
1. Early Judean Ministry	4:12	1:14a	3:19–20, 4:14a	1:19–4:4
2. Samaritan Ministry				4:5–45
3. Early Galilean Ministry	4:13–25, 8:2–4, 8:14–17, 9:1–17, 12:1–21	1:14b–3:12	4:14b–6:11	4:46–5:47
4. Middle Galilean Ministry	5:1–8:1; 8:5–13, 18, 23–34; 9:18–11:30; 12:22–15:20	3:13–7:23	6:12–9:17	6:1–-7:1
5. Later Galilean Ministry	15:21–18:35	7:24–9:50	9:18–50	

Harmony of the Gospels (Simplified)

	Matthew	Mark	Luke	John
6. Later Judean Ministry	8:19–22	10:1a	9:51–13:21	7:2—10:39
7. Perean Ministry	19:1—20:34; 26:6–13	10:1b–52, 14:3–9	13:22—19:28	10:40—12:11
Trials Period				
1. Sunday	21:1–11, 14–17	11:1–11	19:29–44	12:12–19
2. Monday	21:12–13, 18–19a	11:12–18	19:45–48	12:20–50
3. Tuesday	21:19b-25:46	11:19–13:37	20:1–21:38	
4. Wednesday	26:1–5, 14–16	14:1–2, 10–11	22:1–6	
5. Thursday	26:17–75	14:12–72	22:7–65	13:1–18:27
6. Friday	27:1–60	15:1–47	22:66–23:56	18:28–19:42
7. Saturday	27:61–66	16:1		
Triumphant Period				
1. Absence from the tomb	28:1–8	16:2–8	24:1–12	20:1–10
2. Appearances	28:9–20	16:9–18	24:13–49	20:11–21:25
3. Ascension		16:19–20	24:50–53	

Appendix C

The John 3:16 One Verse Method
Helping Others Believe in Jesus

THE STRUCTURE OF THIS method is designed to help you with both what to say and what to do in guiding another person through the message of John 3:16. At each step, clearly identified sections *(Transition and Explanation)* give you an example of what to say in transitioning into and explaining each aspect of believing in Jesus. Please feel free to personalize these transitions and explanations. Do not try to memorize the exact wording. Each step also includes a section *(Action)* which describes what to write or draw on a piece of paper as you give the corresponding explanation.

Introducing The Verse

Transition

Do you feel like you have a personal relationship with God or do you feel like you're still in the process? May I explain to you what the Bible says about entering into a personal relationship with God?

Action

Take a piece of paper (or a napkin) and write the words of John 3:16 at the very top of the sheet in this particular order. (To help you remember this order, note that the middle two phrases both start with the word "that" and both end with a reference to Jesus Christ.) Number these phrases in the following order: 1,3,4,2.

John 3:16

1) For God so loved the world
3) that He gave His only begotten Son
4) that whoever believes in Him
2) should not perish but have eternal life.

Explanation

Many people have heard of this verse. The reason John 3:16 is so famous is because it summarizes the core message of the Bible in four spiritual truths.

God's Purpose

Transition

Let's look at the first truth. What does God desire from man?

Action

Put quotation marks around the words "God," "loved," and "world." About halfway down the page, begin to diagram this truth by writing the word "God" on the right, the word "world" on the left, and the word "love" down the middle.

John 3:16

1) For "God" so "loved" the "world"
3) that He gave His only begotten Son
4) that whoever believes in Him
2) should not perish but have eternal life.

```
WORLD            L               GOD
                 O
                 V
                 E
```

Explanation

God created people to have a personal relationship with Him. He wants this relationship to be one of love—one where God shows His love to people and where people show their love to Him.

Man's Problem

Transition

Let's look at the second spiritual truth. Why do you think more people are not experiencing this loving personal relationship?

Action

Write the word "sin" below the word "love." Then draw two cliffs, one under the word "world," and one under the word "God."

John 3:16

1) For "God" so "loved" the "world"
3) that He gave His only begotten Son
4) that whoever believes in Him
2) should not perish but have eternal life.

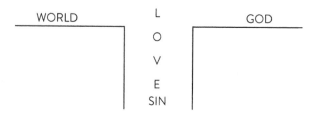

Explanation

It is because of sin. Sin is disobeying God. When someone is offended it causes problems in the relationship. A person's sin, whether in action or attitude, causes a separation between Holy God and man. The Bible calls this separation spiritual death.

Transition

It's bad enough to be separated from God because of our sin, but it gets worse.

Action

Put quotation marks around the word "perish" and write it under the left-hand cliff (the one with the word "world" on it). Draw an arrow downward from the word "perish" and write the word "hell."

John 3:16

1) For "God" so "loved" the "world"
3) that He gave His only begotten Son
4) that whoever believes in Him
2) should not "perish" but have eternal life.

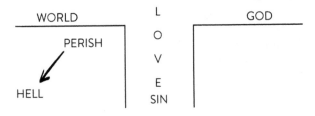

Explanation

The Bible says that if anyone dies physically while separated from God spiritually, he/she will spend eternity in a place called hell.

Transition

That's bad news, but this second spiritual truth also gives hope.

Action

Put quotation marks around the words "eternal life" and write them under the right-hand cliff. Draw an arrow downward from the words "eternal life" and write the word "heaven."

John 3:16

1) For "God" so "loved" the "world"
3) that He gave His only begotten Son
4) that whoever believes in Him
2) should not "perish" but have "eternal life. "

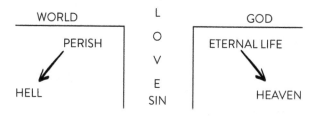

Explanation

God does not want man to spend eternity in hell because of his sin. God desires to have a personal relationship with man so that they can live together forever in a place called heaven.

God's Remedy

Transition

The question then becomes: How does one deal with this problem of sin? That leads us to the third spiritual truth.

Action

Put quotation marks around the word "Son" and write it on the diagram so that it shares the "o" of the word "love." Then draw a cross that encloses the words "Son" and "love" and bridges the two cliffs.

John 3:16

1) For "God" so "loved" the "world"
3) that He gave His only begotten "Son"
4) that whoever believes in Him
2) should not "perish" but have "eternal life. "

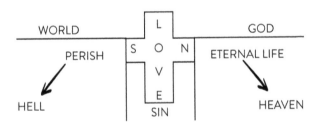

Explanation

God took care of the sin problem by sending His Son, Jesus Christ, to eliminate the separation between us and God. After living a perfect life for 33 years, Christ was willingly crucified on a cross to pay the penalty for our sins. After He was buried, to the shock of those who loved Him and those who hated Him, He rose from the dead. This resulted immediately in two accomplishments: sin was paid for and a bridge between us and God was established.

Man's Response

Transition

The question now is: How can a person cross over the bridge that Christ has provided and personally experience God's love and forgiveness? The fourth spiritual truth gives the answer.

Action

Draw an arching arrow from the word "world" to the word "God." Put quotation marks around the words "believes in Him" and write them on the arrow as shown.

John 3:16

1) For "God" so "loved" the "world"
3) that He gave His only begotten "Son"
4) that whoever "believes in Him"
2) should not "perish" but have "eternal life. "

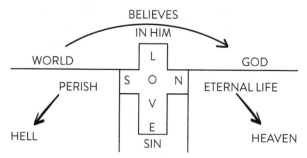

Explanation

Most people think a person crosses over by being good. Yet, one could never be good enough to get to Holy God. Crossing over into a right relationship with God comes by trusting Christ to take you across, rather than by trying to get across through your own efforts. A right relationship with God is received from Christ by faith, not achieved for Christ by works.

Inviting a Decision

Transition

May we personalize this for a moment?

Action

Draw a circle around the word "whoever."

John 3:16

1) For "God" so "loved" the "world"
3) that He gave His only begotten "Son"
4) that <u>whoever</u> "believes in Him"
2) should not "perish" but have "eternal life. "

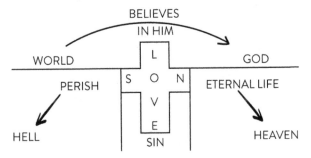

Explanation

Where would you put yourself on this diagram?

- If they put themselves on the right-hand side, ask them to tell you when they crossed over.

- If they put themselves on the left-hand side, or on top of the cross, ask the next question:

Do you see anything keeping you from trusting Christ to take you across to God right now?

- If they say "yes", ask them what their questions are and deal with them accordingly. If you do not know the answer to a question, tell them you will try to find out and get back to them with the answer.

- If they say "no", prepare to lead them in prayer expressing their desire to God.

Guiding in Prayer

Transition

If you desire to trust Christ to make you right with God, you can do so right now.

Action

In the diagram, place the number "1" next the word "God", the number "2" next to the word "world", the number "3", next to the cross, and the number "4" beside the word "believes."

John 3:16

1) For "God" so "loved" the "world"
3) that He gave His only begotten "Son"
4) that <u>whoever</u> "believes in Him"
2) should not "perish" but have "eternal life. "

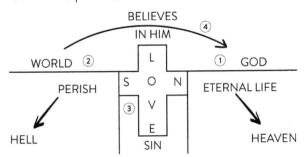

Explanation

You can express your trust in Christ by telling God: (1) that you are thankful that He loves you; (2) that you are sorry for your sin which has separated you from Him; (3) that you are grateful that He gave His only Son to forgive your sin and give you eternal life; and (4) that you believe Christ will make you right with Him, right now.

I can pray and you can repeat after me. Remember, what is most important is the attitude of your heart, not the words of your mouth. You can pray the right words, but if your heart is not truly convinced that only Christ can make you right with God, then you will not cross over to God. Let's pray. (Pray the above four truths to God, pausing so the seeker can pray after you.)